THE SMITH KIDS, THANKS FOR READING. I REALLY LIKE HAVING YOU ALONG!

For my grand kids to see where I worked as the American Exchange Scientist with the British Antarctic Survey, 1962-63

3-29-2008

Barrington Bear Visits the Emperor

Dedicated to Young Readers Everywhere

BARRINGTON BEAR

Books in the Travels with Barrington Bear Series

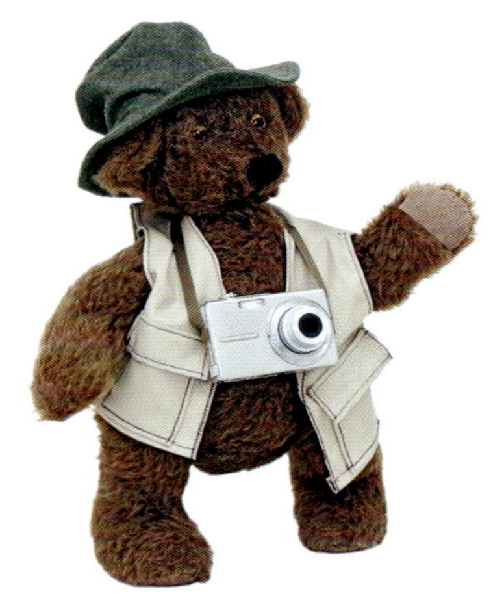

Barrington Bear Visits the Emperor

Barrington Bear on Safari

BOOK ONE IN THE TRAVELS WITH BARRINGTON BEAR SERIES

Barrington Bear Visits the Emperor

The Emperor Penguin That Is

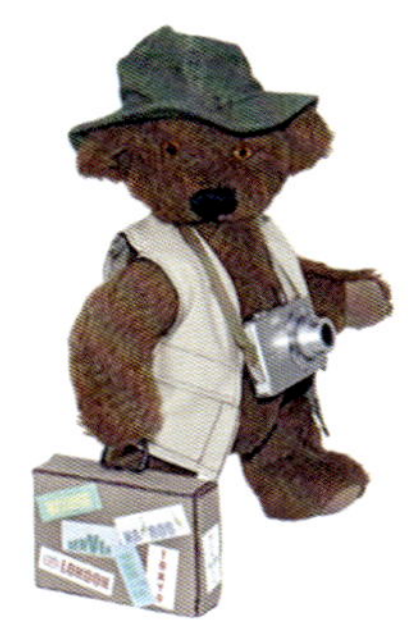

A Beary Exciting Story by KEITH SZAFRANSKI

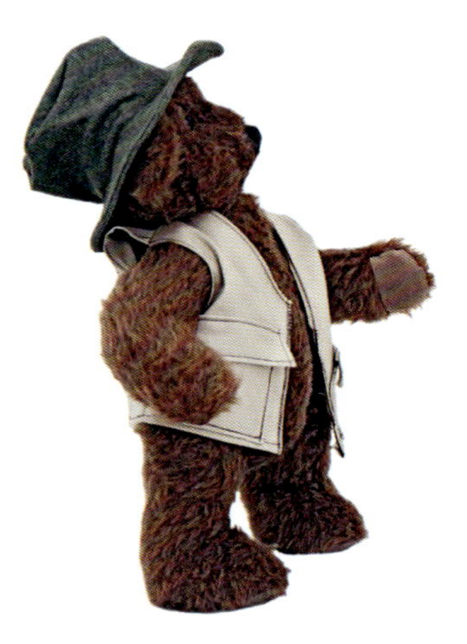

Small Bear Publishing
P. O. Box 842
Livingston, MT 59047

Barrington also has his own website: www.travelswithbarrington.com
and an email address: barringtonbear@q.com

Printed in the United States of America

ISBN: 978-0-9801662-0-0

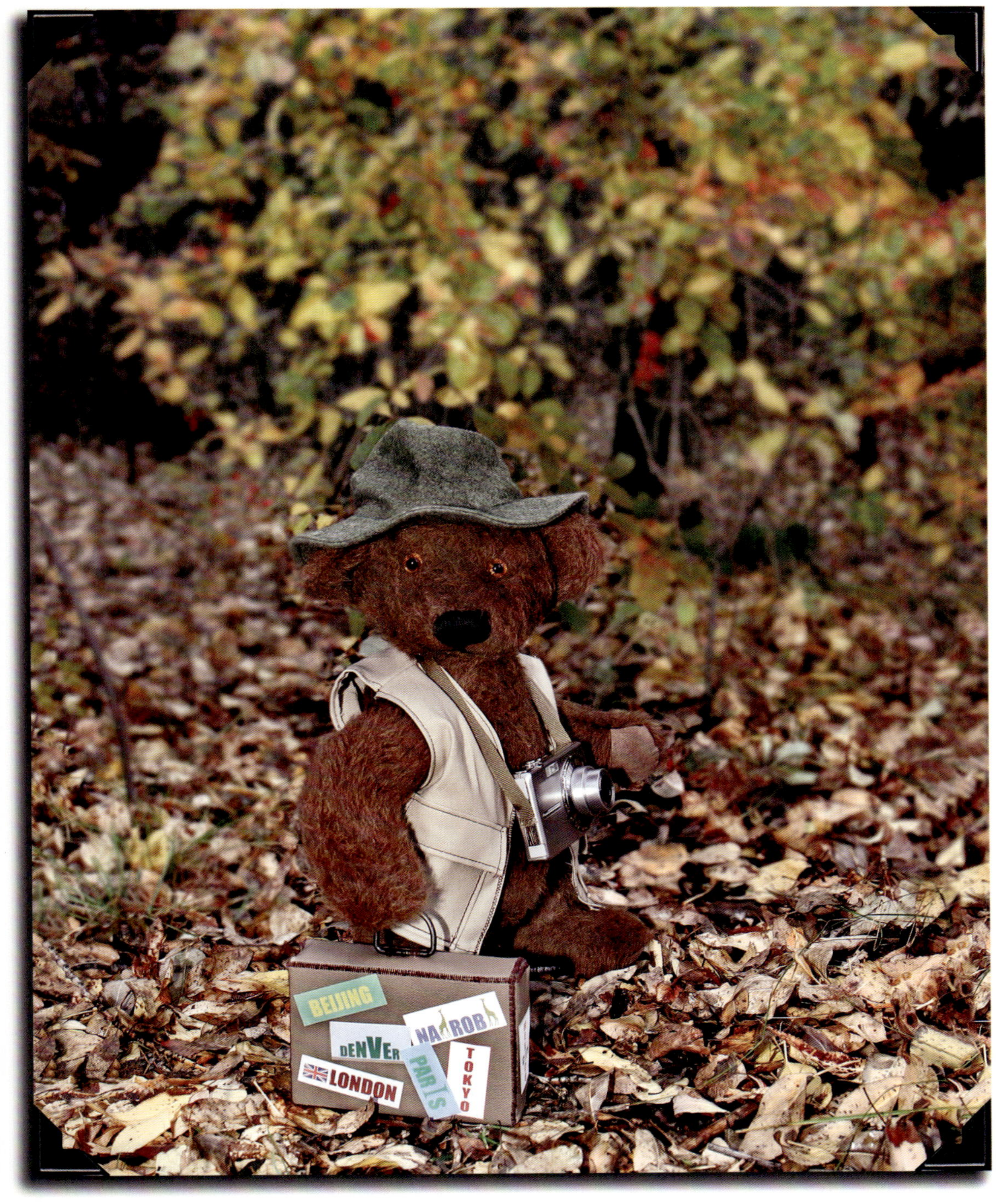

It's October.
Most bears are getting ready for a long winter's nap. But Barrington Bear is ready for a trip. His suitcase is packed. He has his favorite hat. And of course, he couldn't go anywhere without his camera.
"Where are you going this time, Barrington?" his friends ask.
"I am going to visit the Emperor," he replies.
"The Emperor penguin, that is. I am going to Antarctica (ant-ark-tik-a)."
Antarctica is very far away from the Montana woods where Barrington lives.
So...

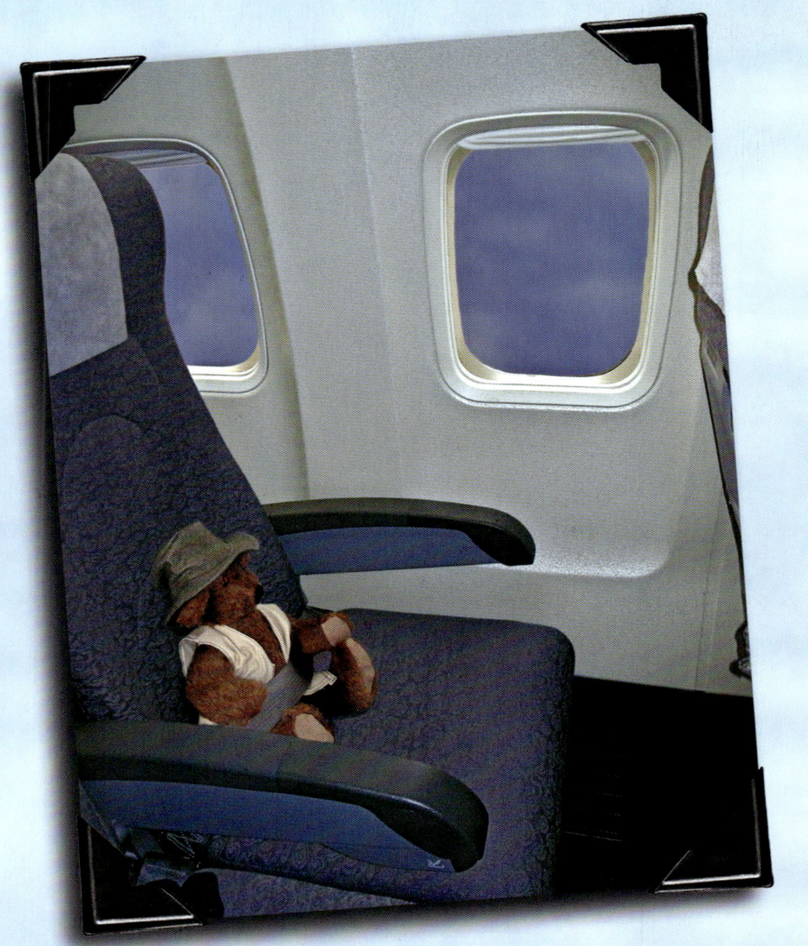

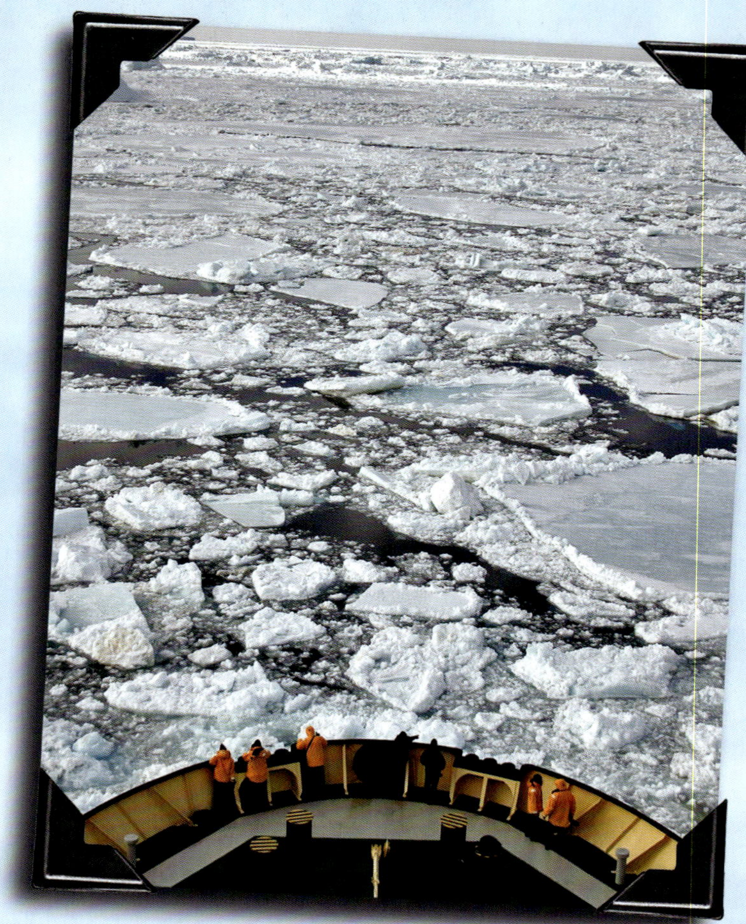

Barrington must first take a long ride on an airplane to Argentina in South America. There he gets on a big ship called an icebreaker. He sails across the frozen ocean to Antarctica.

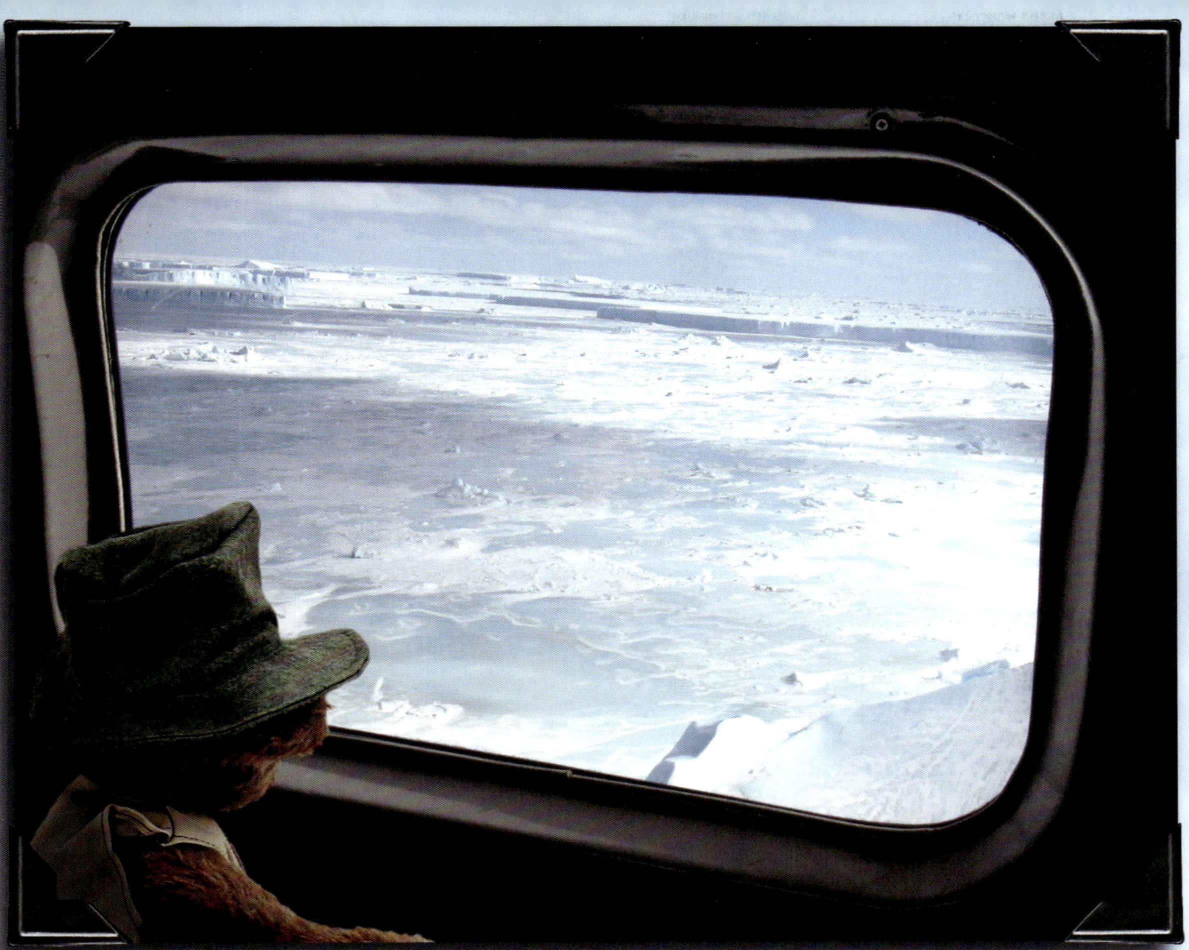

From the ship, Barrington flies in a helicopter. It lands on the ice surrounding Antarctica.

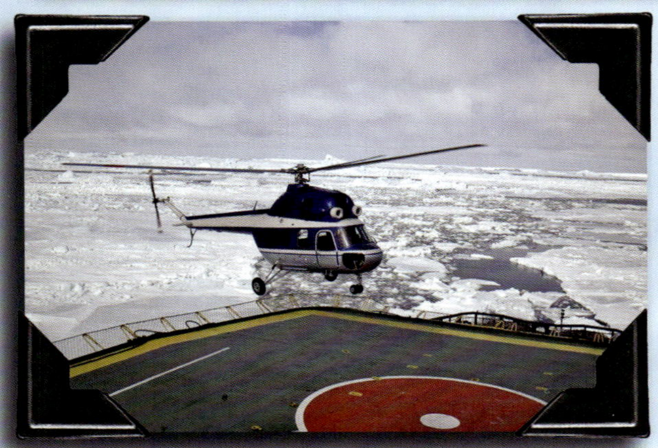

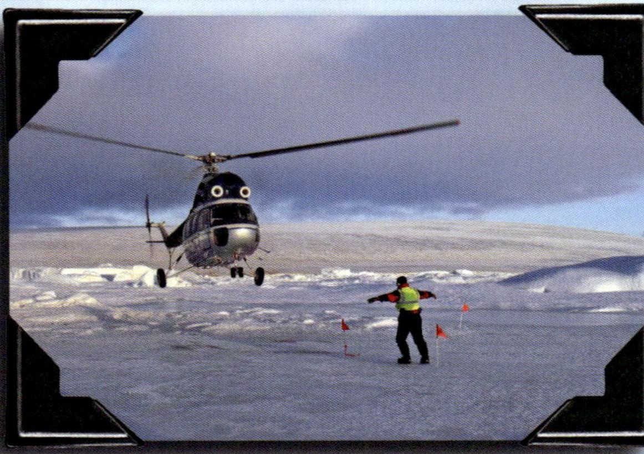

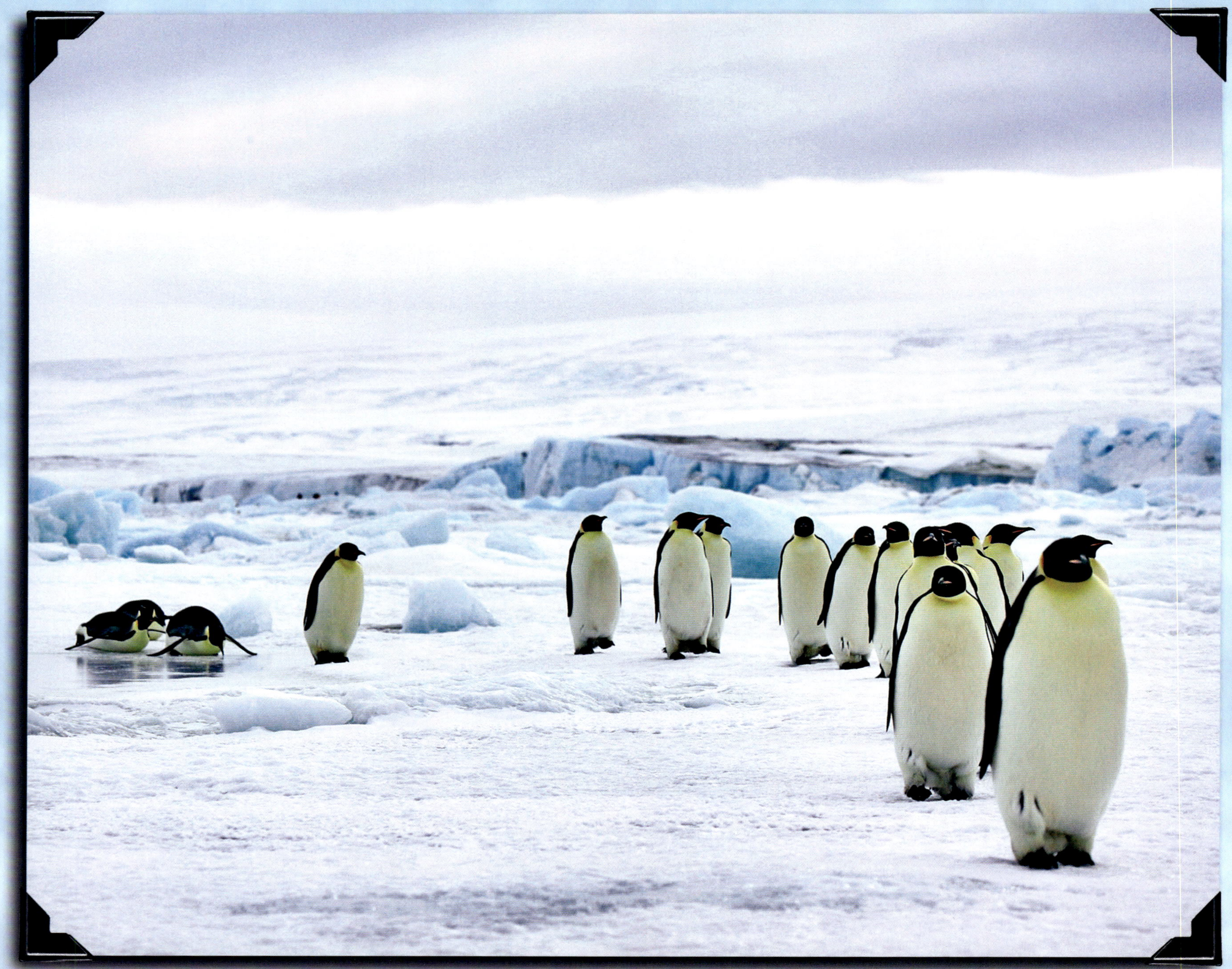

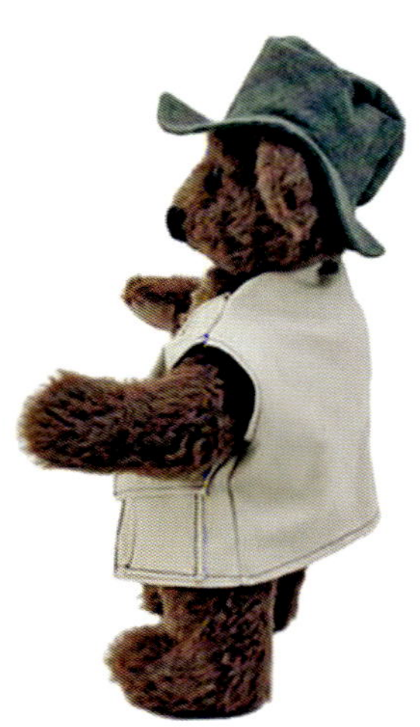

Barrington is not there yet. He walks across the ice in search of the Emperor penguin colony. Along the way he meets several penguins going in the opposite direction.

"Where are you going?" Barrington asks.
"We are looking for a hole in the ice," answers one of the penguins.
"We need to catch fish to bring back to our hungry chicks," says another.
"How do you know which way to go?" asks the bear. "I don't see anything but ice and snow."
"We just know," the penguins reply.

Then they all continue on their search for
a hole
in
the ice.

Barrington Bear continues across the ice
for more than a mile

Then he sees it.

He walks a little farther.

Then he hears it.

Barrington walks a bit more.

Then, he is there.

Penguins as far as he can see—
the Emperor penguin colony at last.

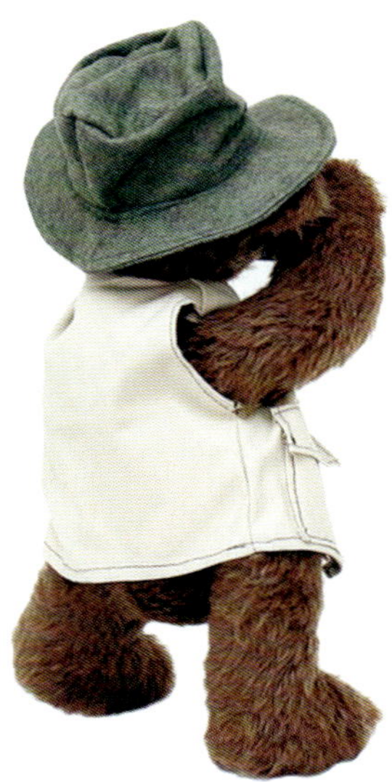

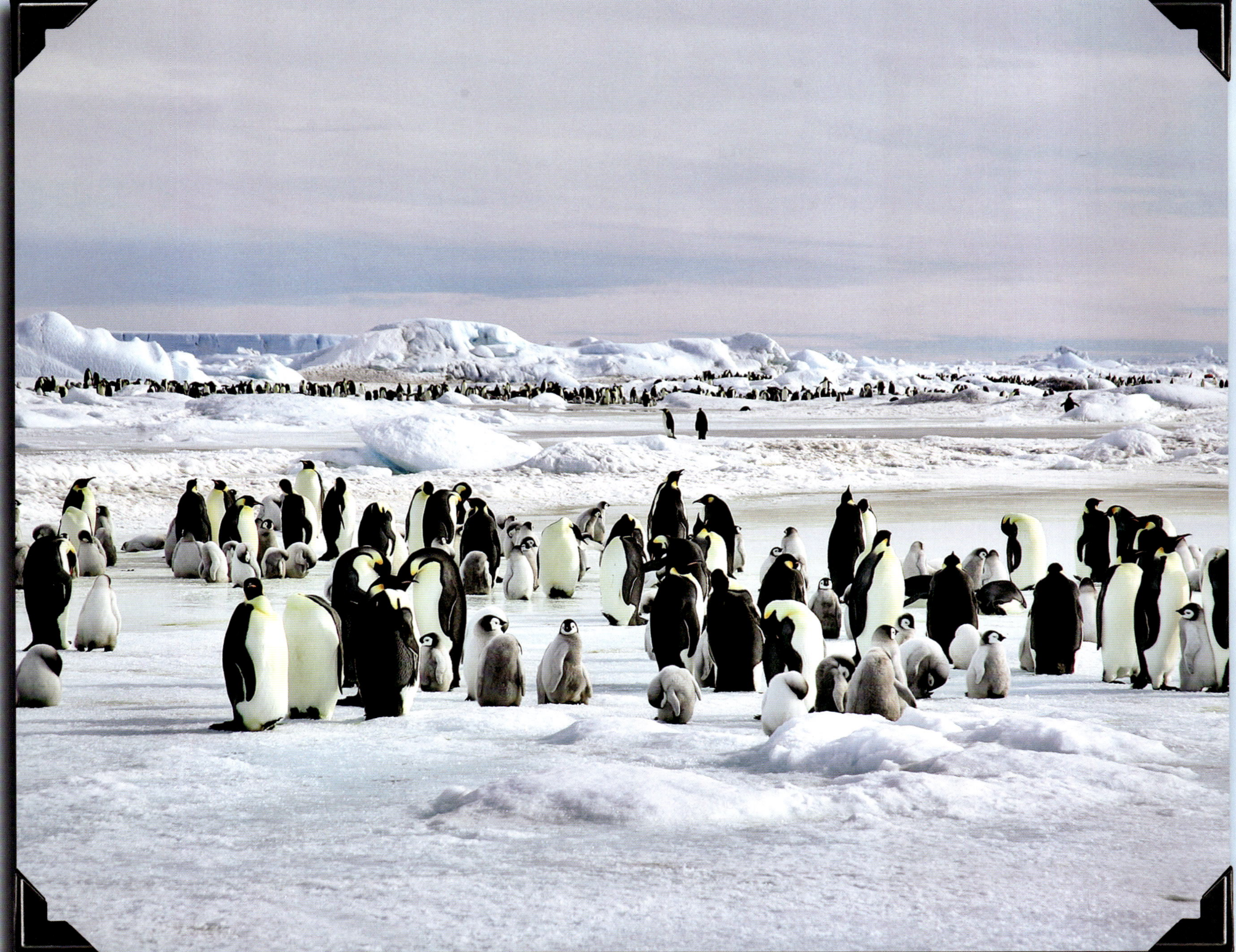

There are thousands of adult penguins. They look like they are ready for a fancy party in their black and white feathers.

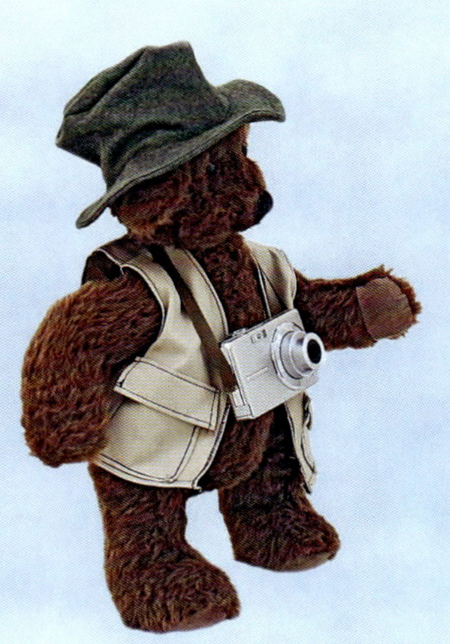

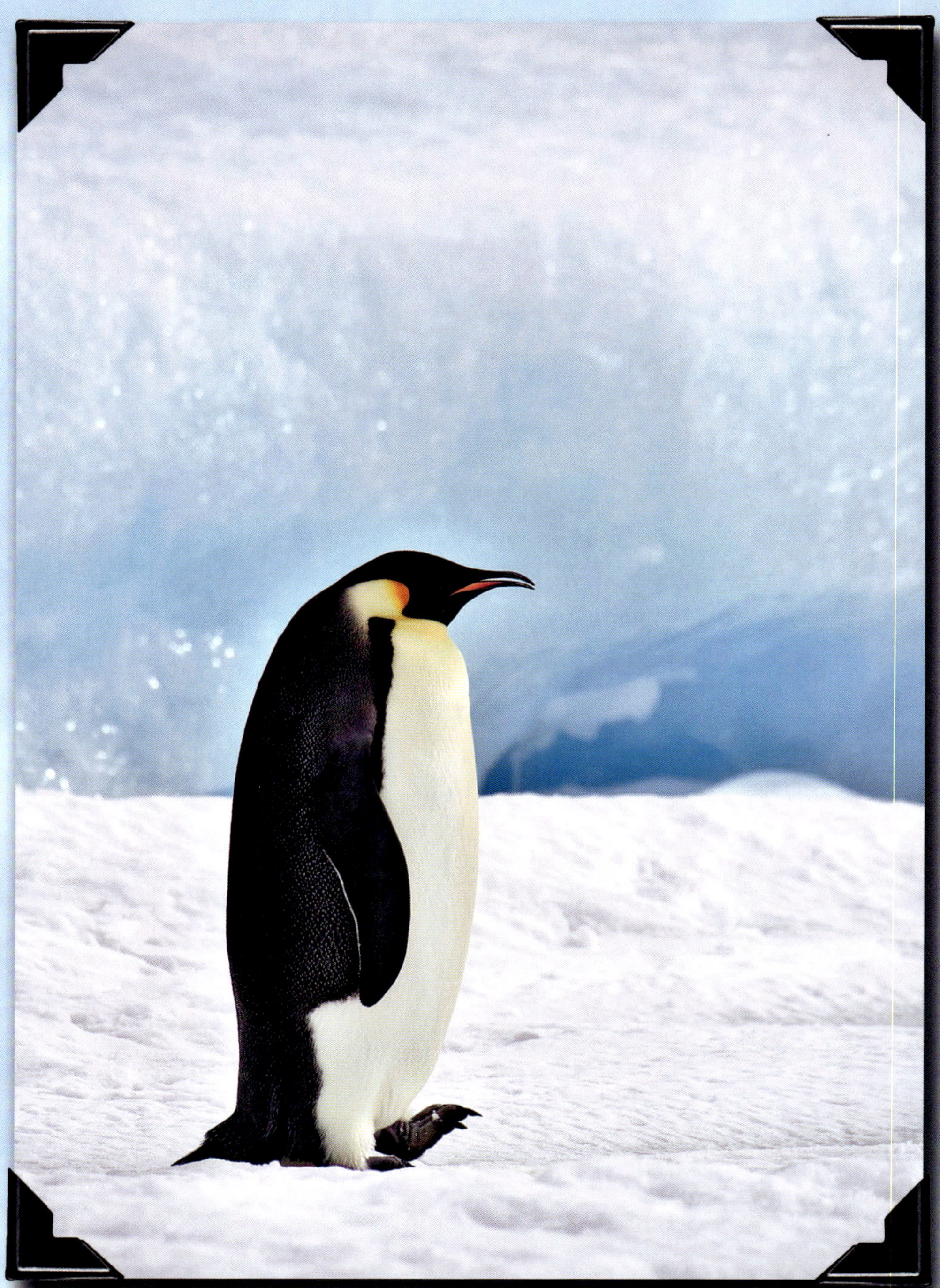

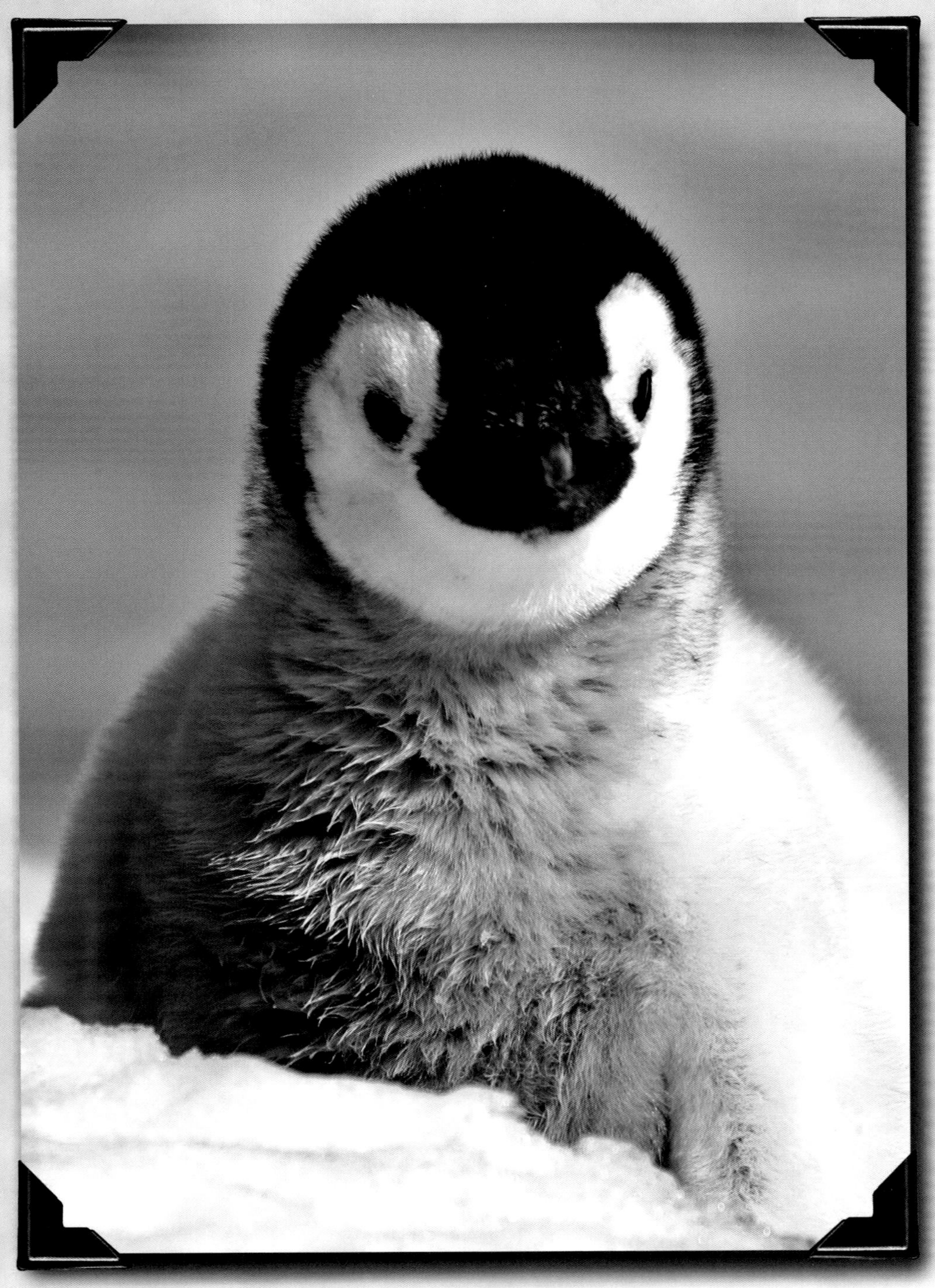

There are also many fat little balls of gray fluff. These are the baby penguins.

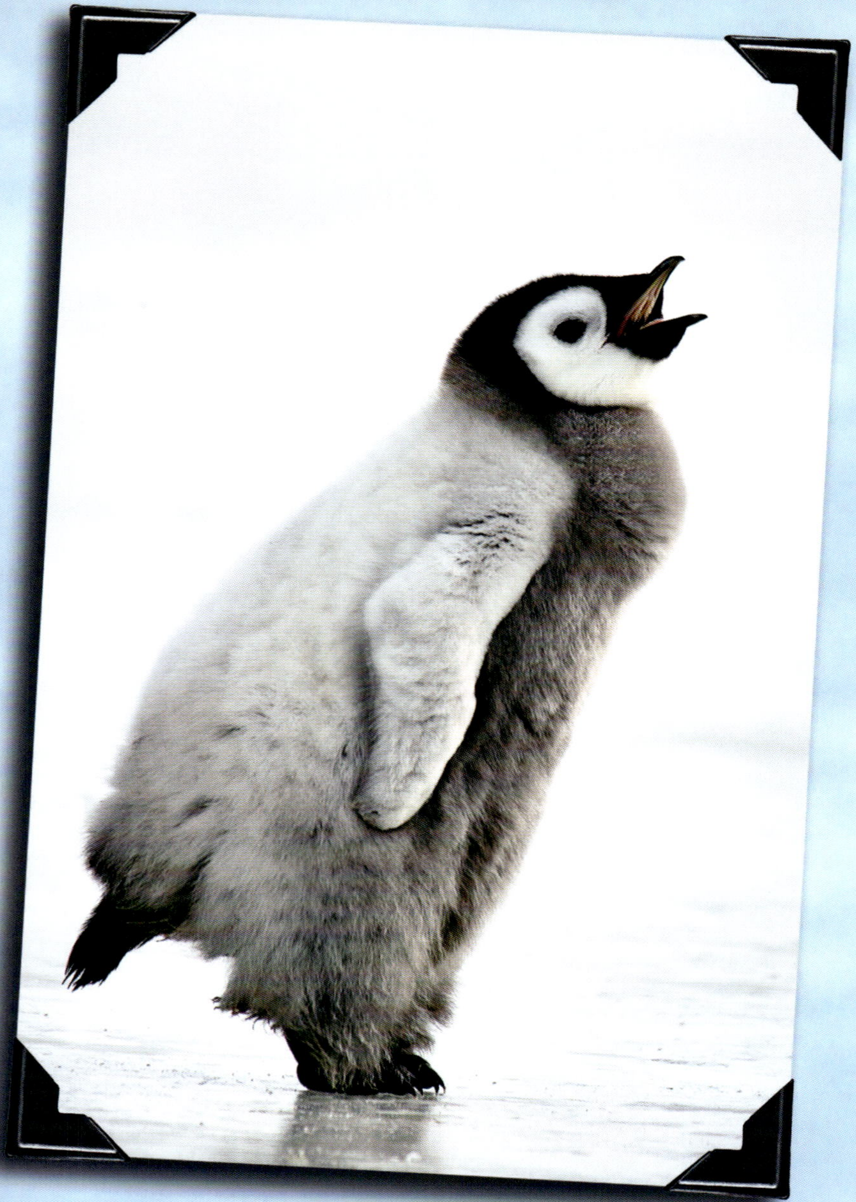

The chicks are calling,
"Sha-weet-weet-werr,"
in a high-pitched voice.

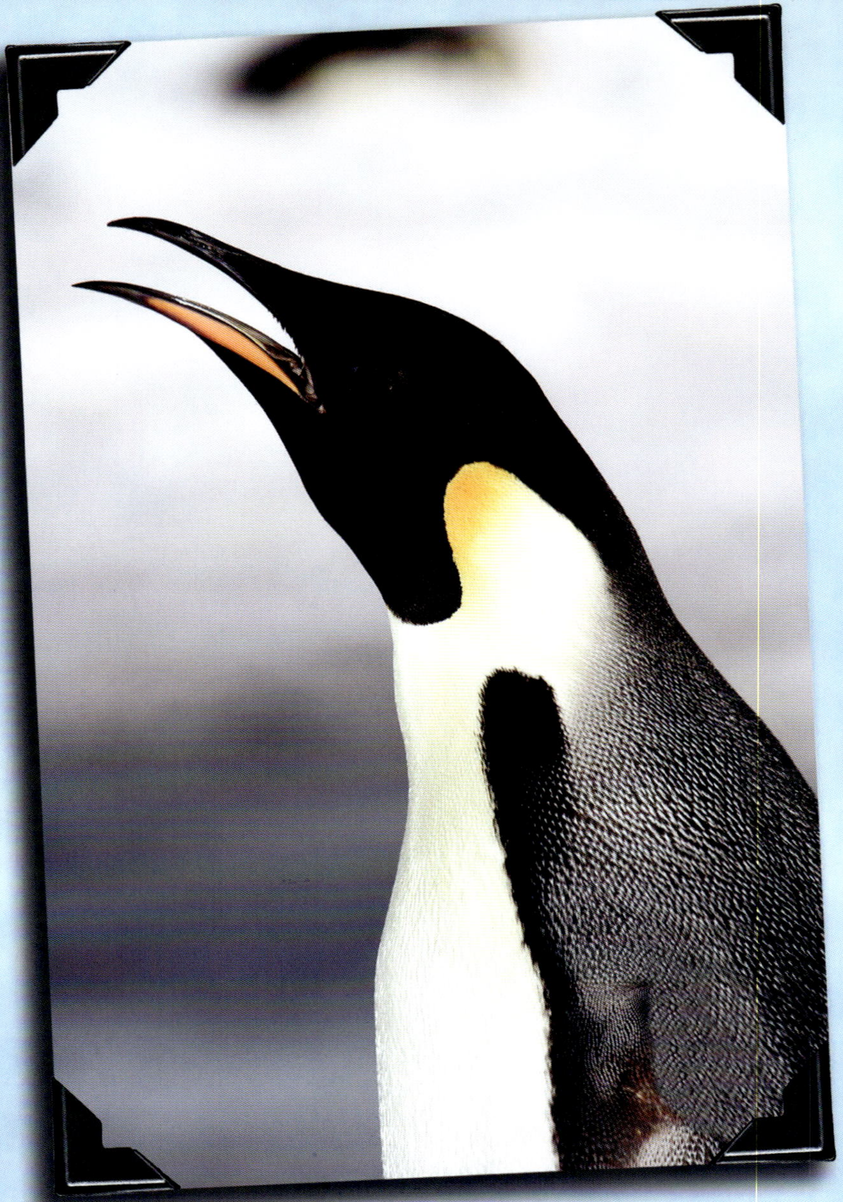

The parents answer,
"Eh-ehhh-eh-eh-ehh-eh-ehhh,"
in a buzzy voice.

"Why are you calling like that?" Barrington asks one of the chicks.

"I am letting my parents know where I am," answers the chick. "They are calling back to let me know that they see me. It makes me feel safe."

"How do you know which call is from your parents?" asks Barrington. "There are so many birds calling. They all sound alike to me."

"I have learned to recognize my parents' voices," replies the chick. "Haven't you?"

Barrington tries to call like a penguin. "AAAAArrrrrrrrr!" roars Barrington.

All of the penguins look scared. Maybe he better not do that again.

Barrington walks around the penguin colony taking pictures.

He takes pictures of the Emperors
doing all sorts of interesting things.

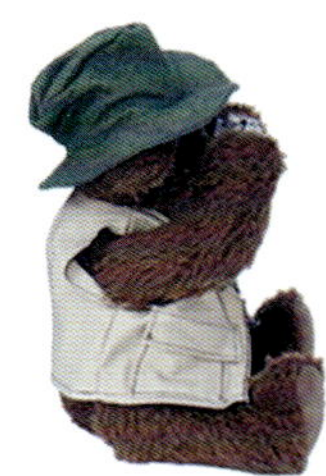

He takes pictures of them resting.

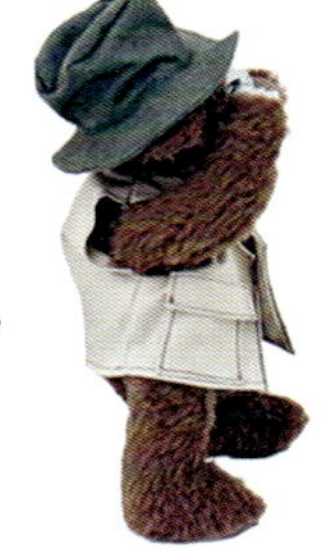

He takes pictures of them walking.

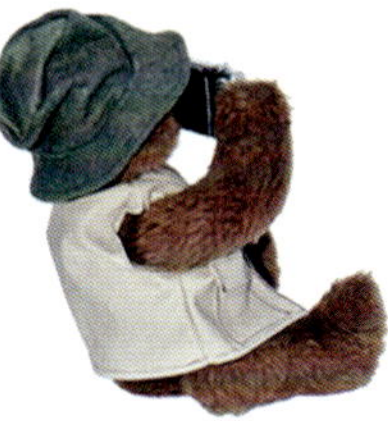

He takes pictures of them preening.

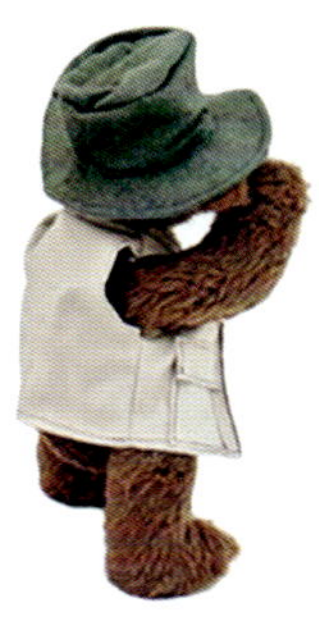

He takes pictures of them scratching.

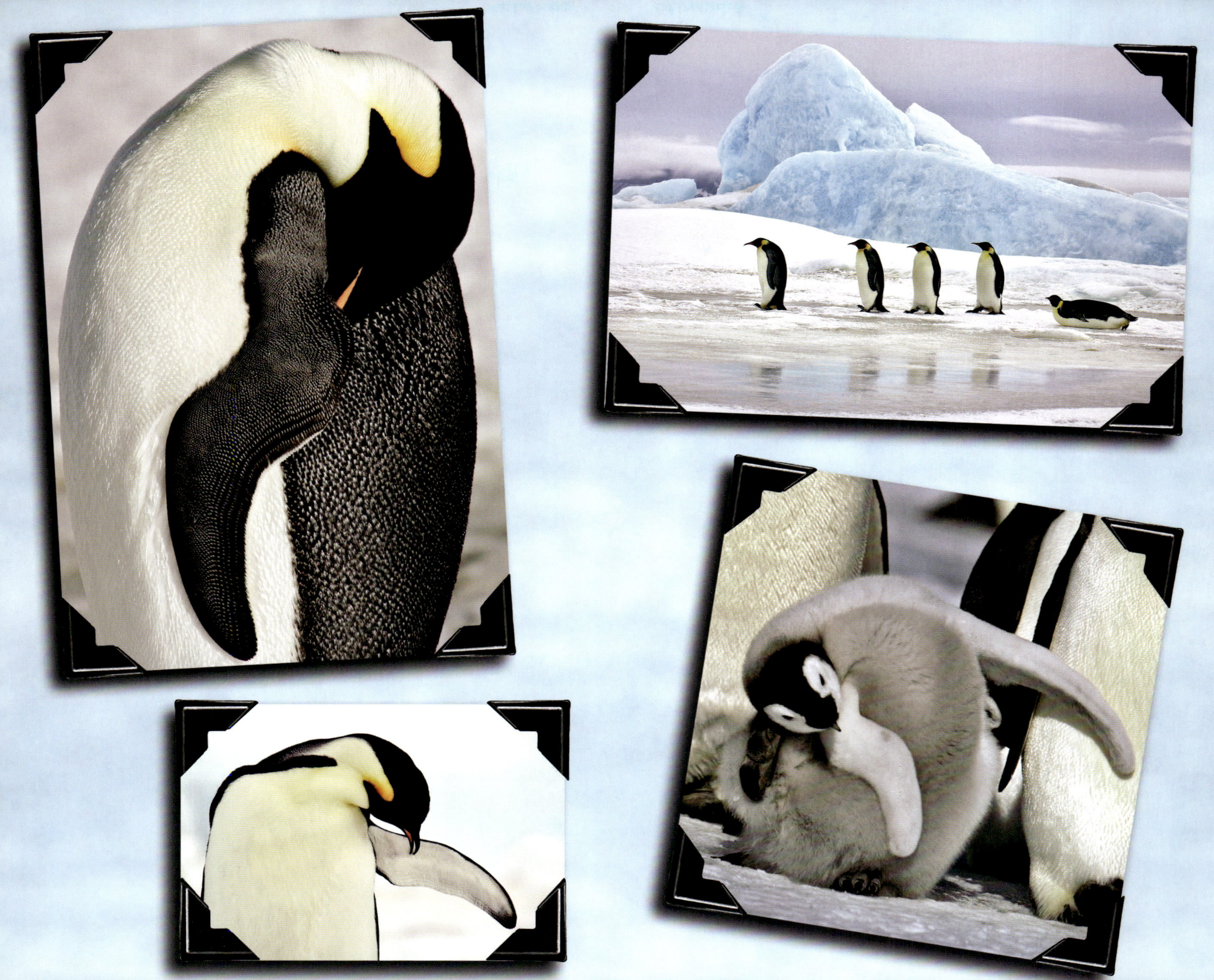

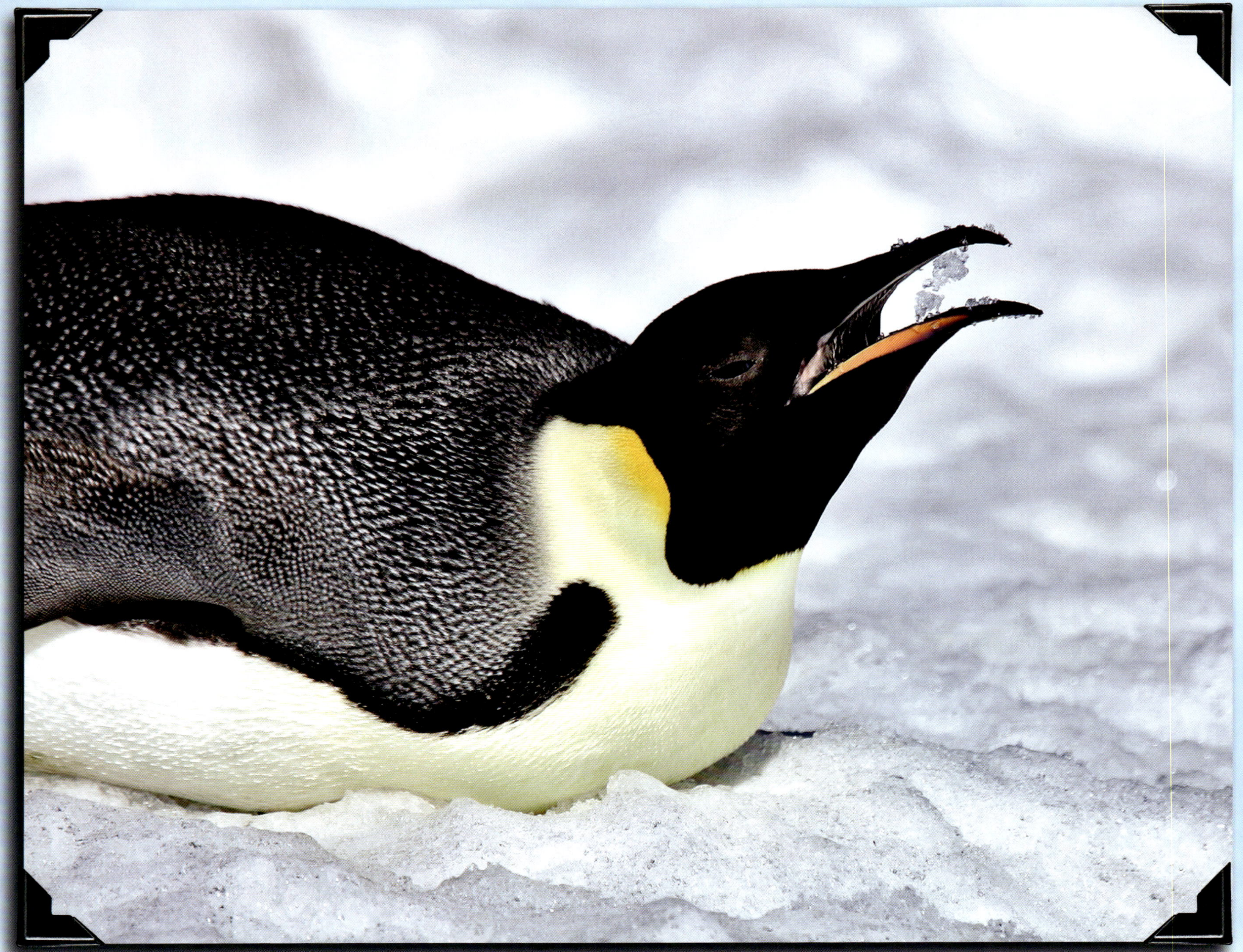

He even takes a picture of a penguin eating ice.

“Why are you eating the ice?” Barrington wants to know.
“I am eating the ice to stay cool,” the penguin answers.
“It is a very warm day.”

“But the temperature is barely above freezing!”
Barrington exclaims.

“To a penguin,” explains the Emperor,
“that IS a very warm day.”

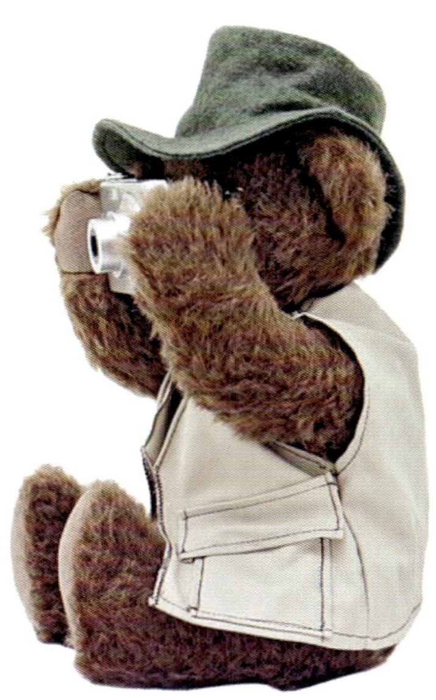

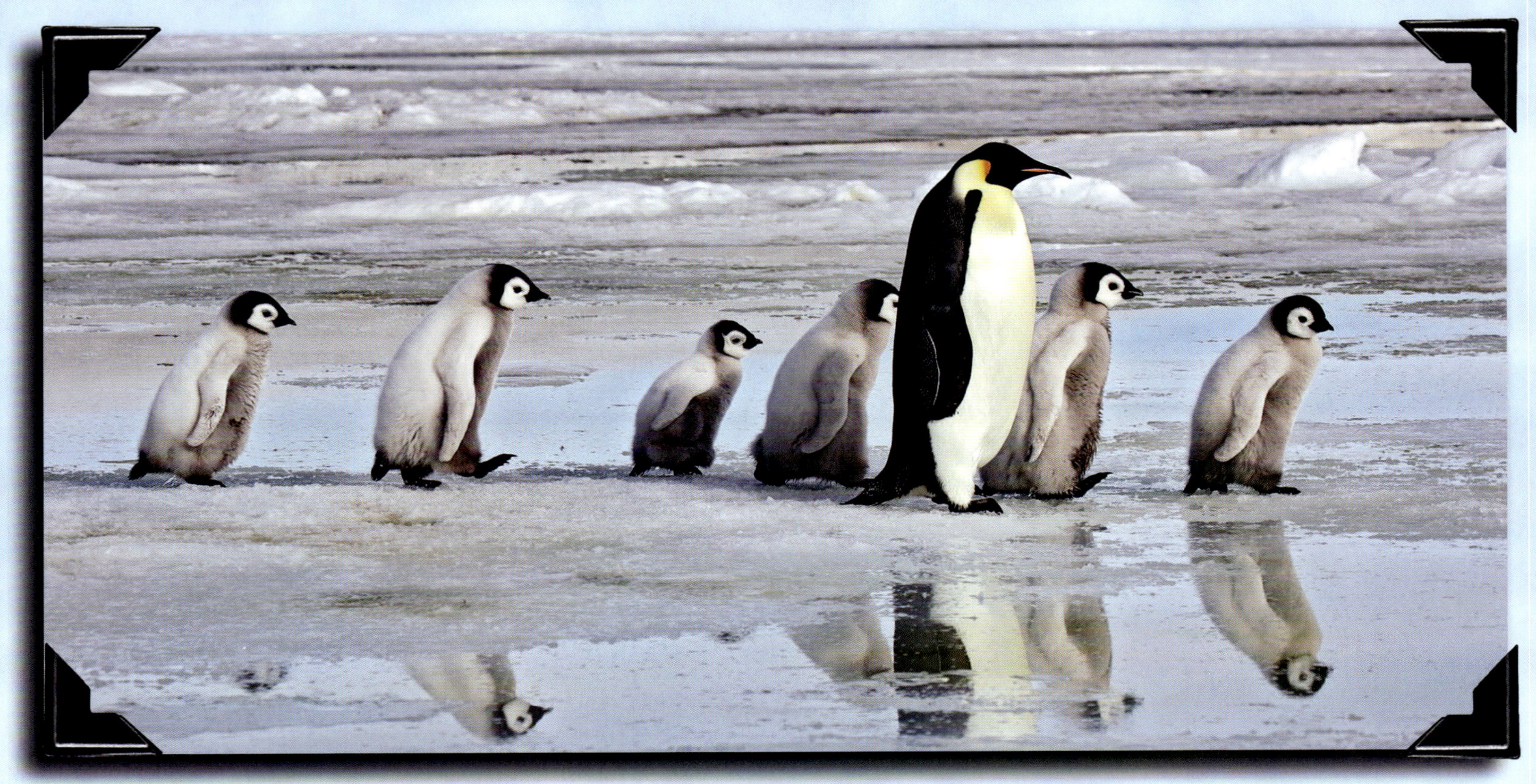

Barrington Bear sees a group of Emperor penguin chicks
following a lone adult bird.
"Is that your babysitter?" Barrington inquires of one of the chicks.
"Sort of," says the chick. "She watches over us
while our parents are away finding food."

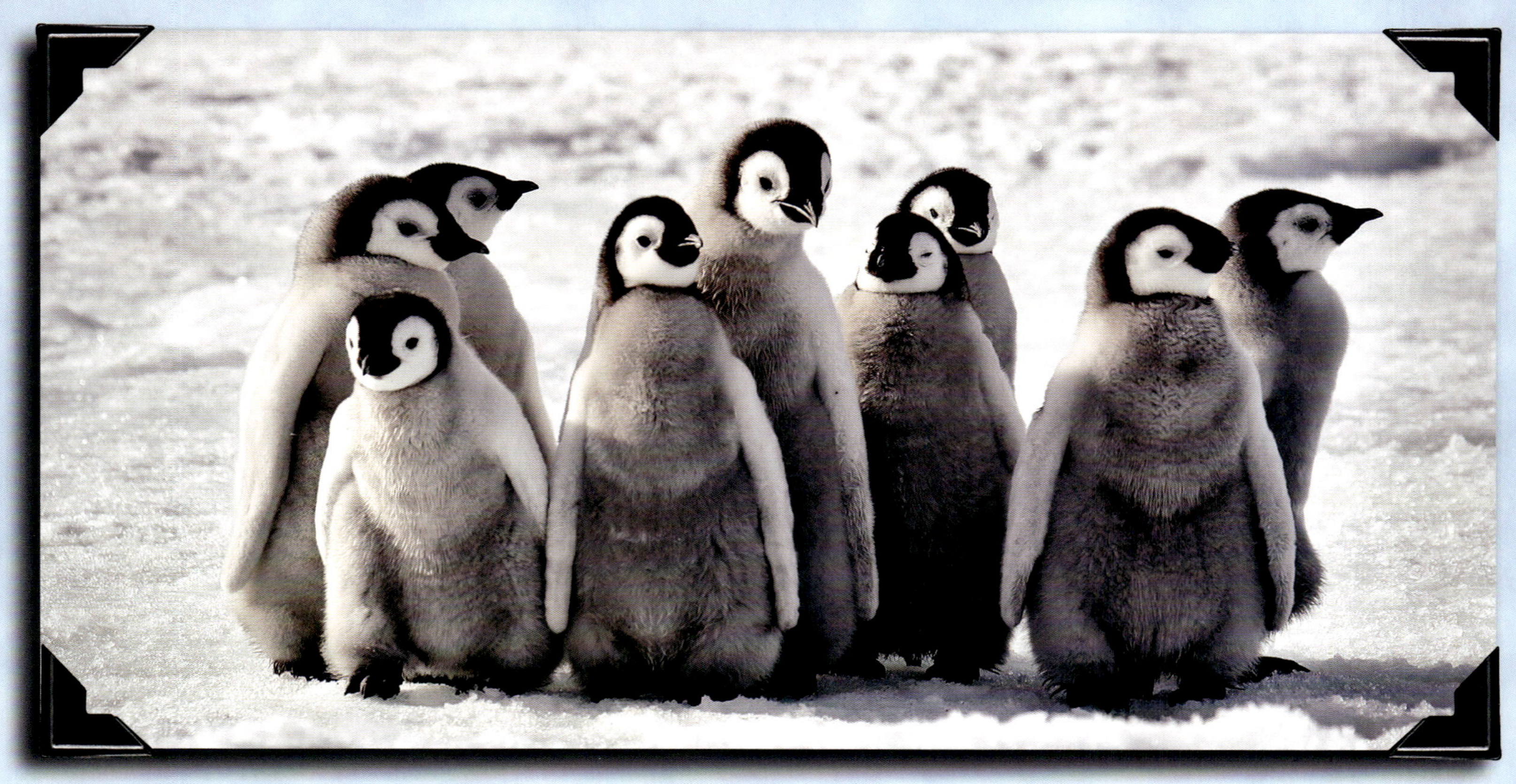

Barrington also notices groups of older chicks all on their own.
Some of the groups are small. Others have dozens of birds.
This is called créching (kreshing).
"We don't like being with adults ALL the time,"
some of the chicks tell Barrington.
"It's fun to hang out with others your own age.
Being in a group also helps to protect us from predators."

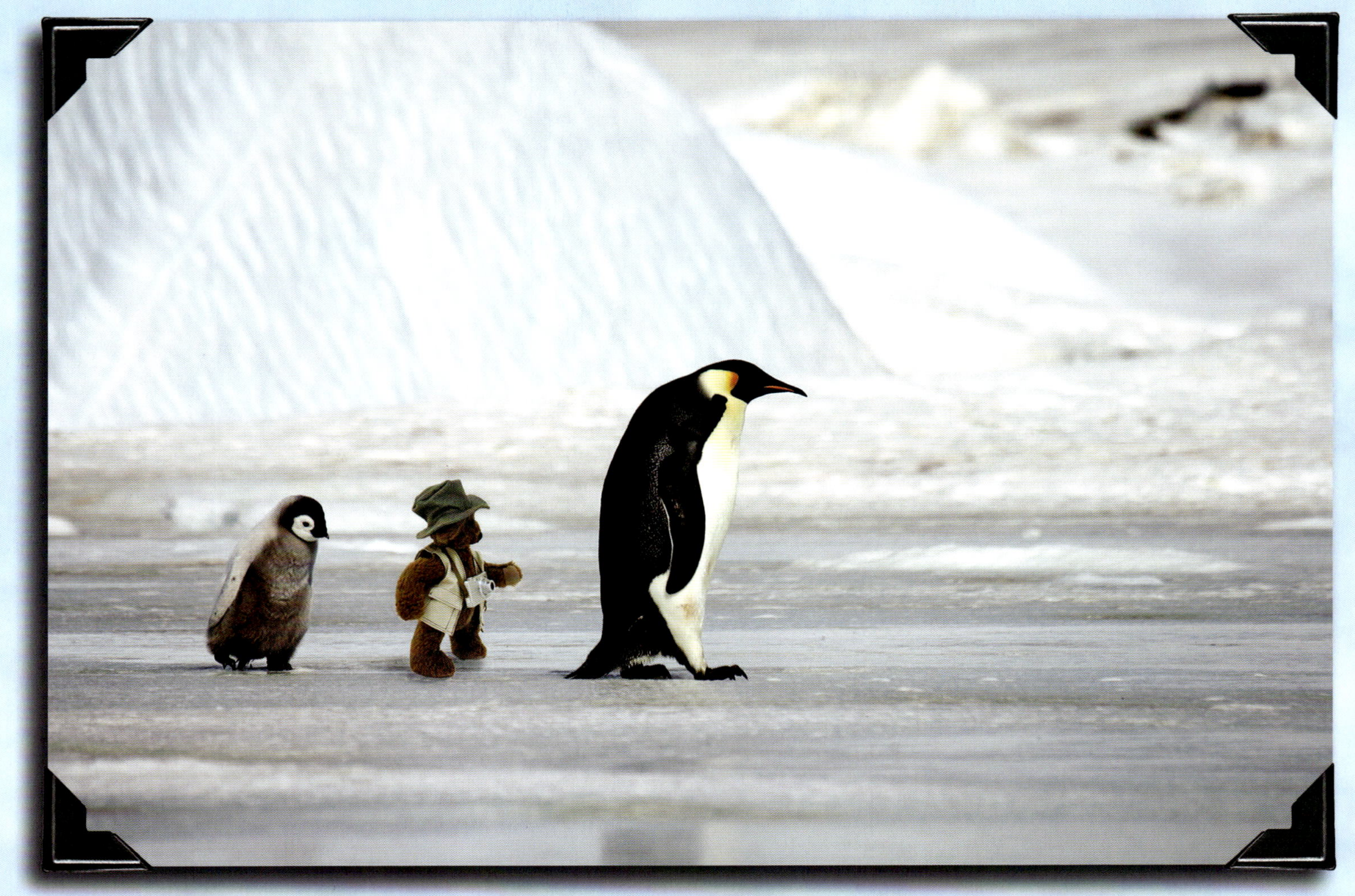

Barrington follows the penguins everywhere.
He takes pictures of everything they do.
He talks with many of them, too.
Barrington learns a lot of interesting things
about Emperor penguins.

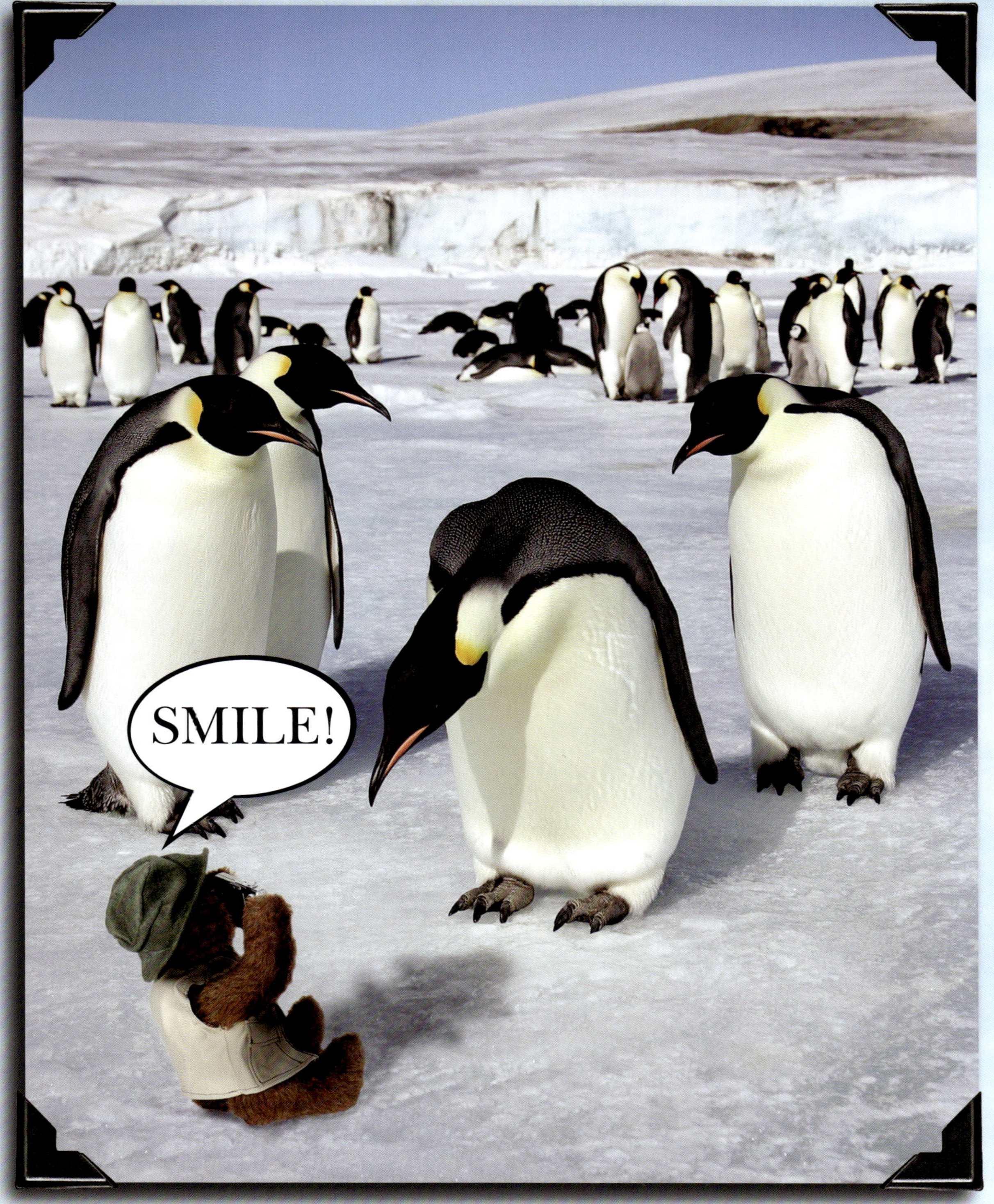

The Emperor penguins are also interested in Barrington.

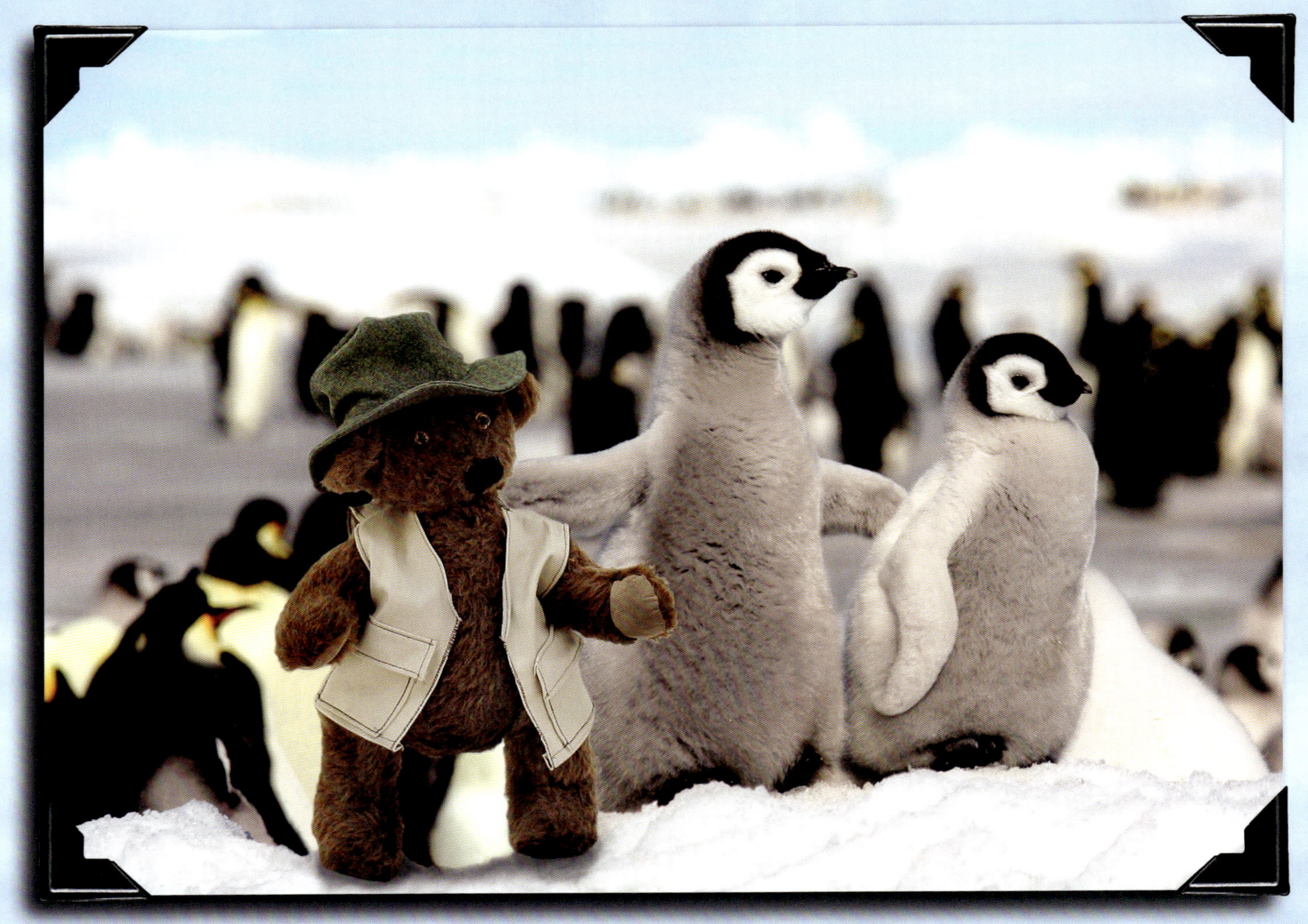

Barrington Bear makes a lot of penguin friends.
Here he poses with two pals for a picture.

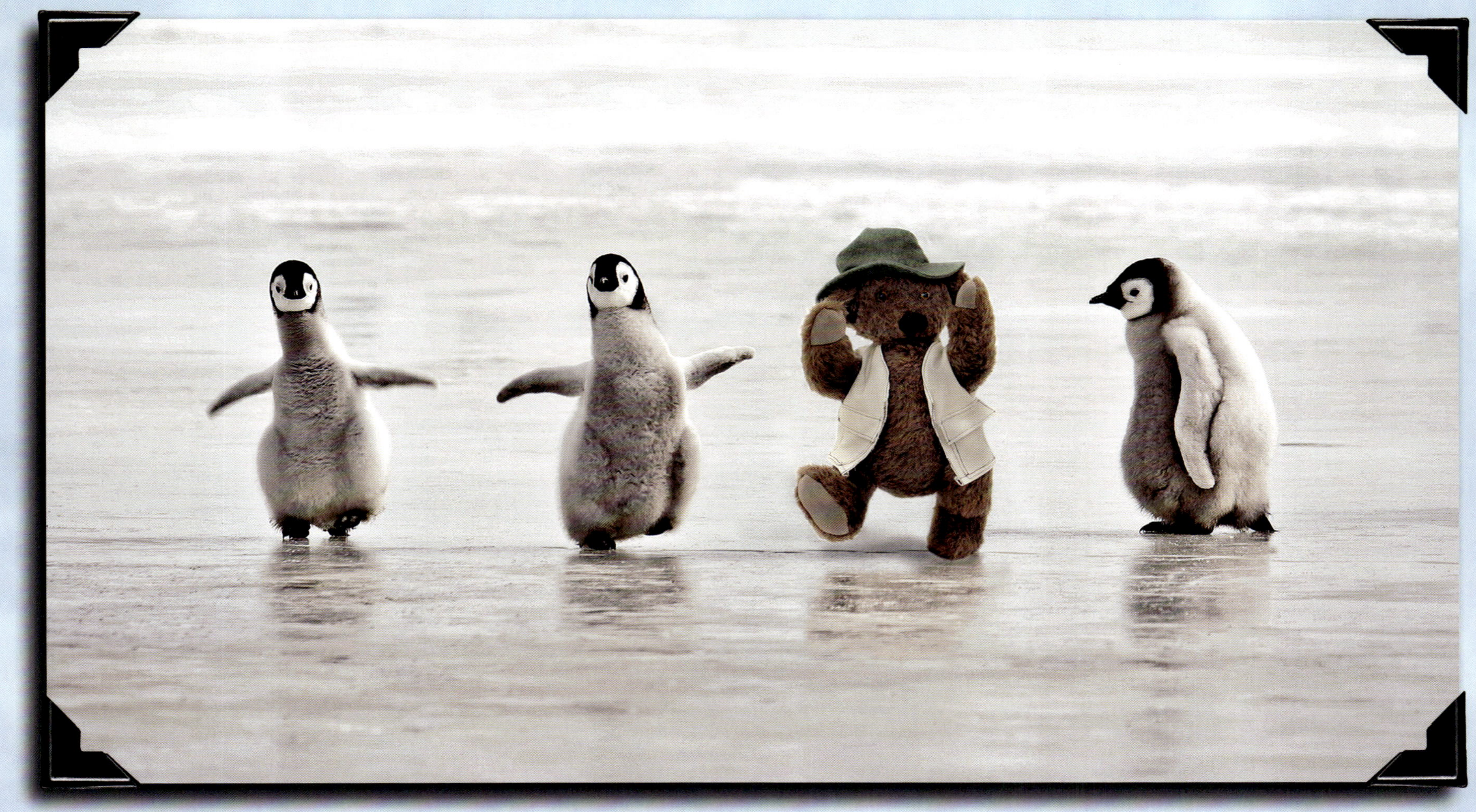

Barrington even joins some of the chicks as they play on the ice.
"Wheeeeeeeeeeeee!"

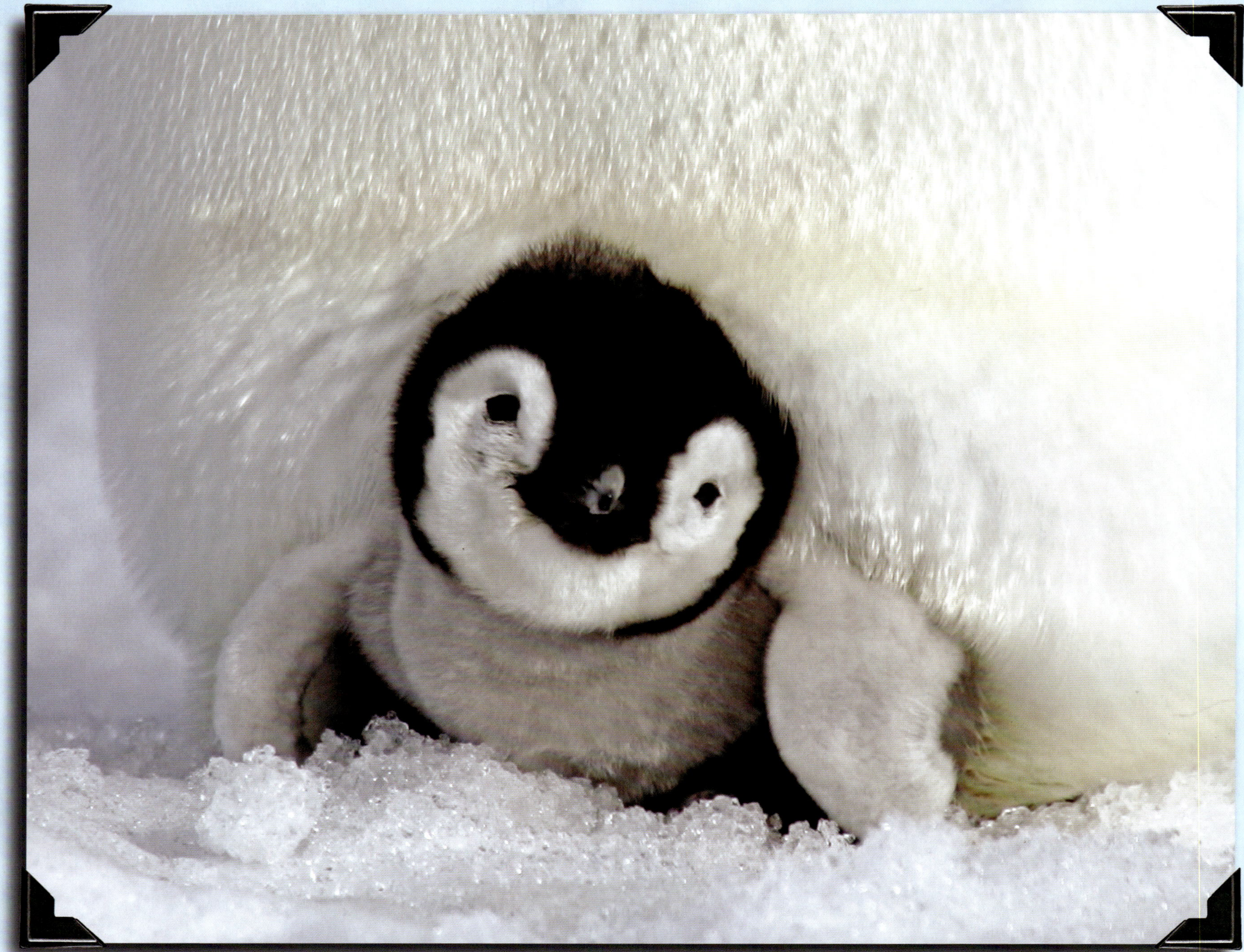

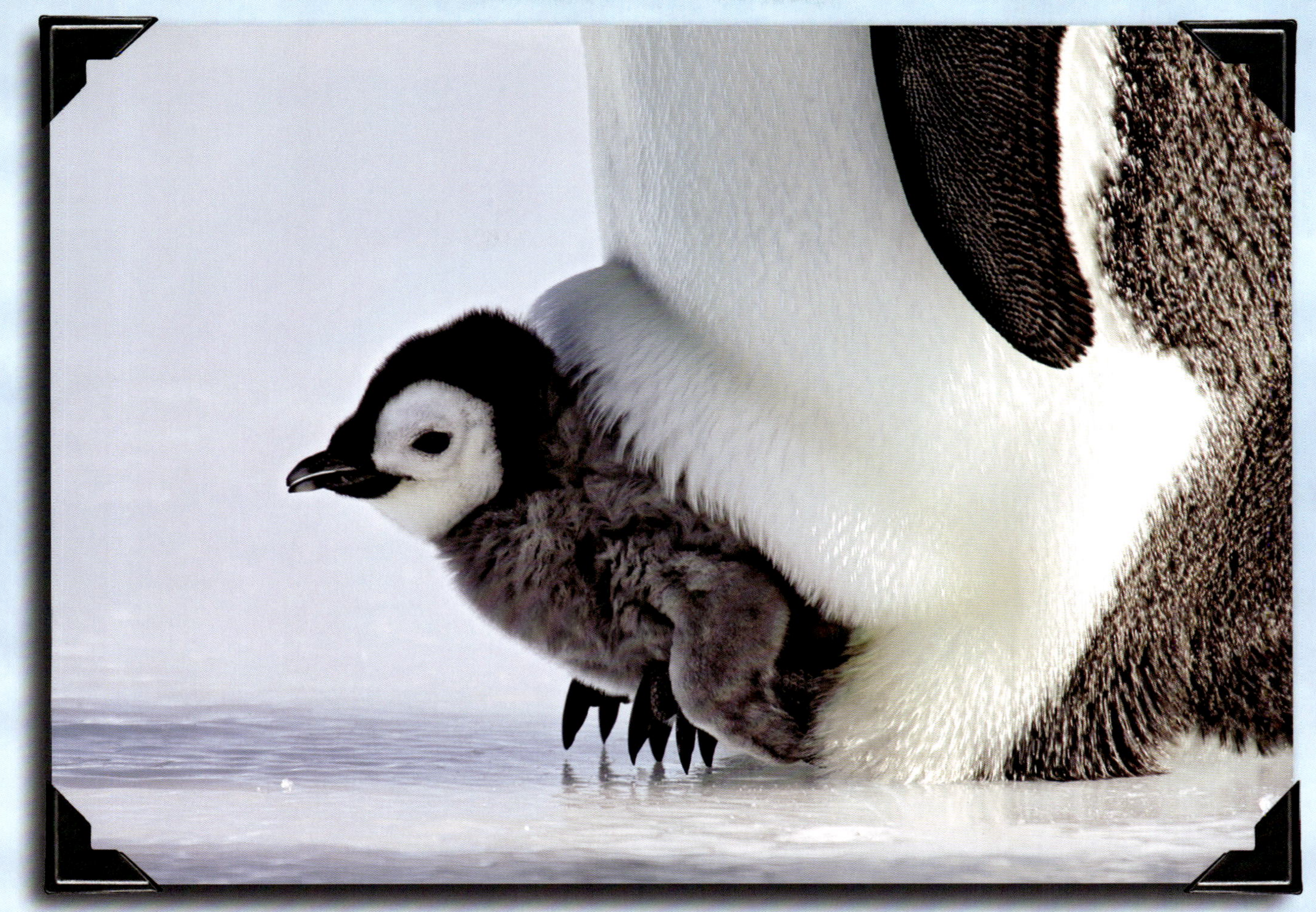

Most of the chicks that Barrington sees are three to four months old.
But Barrington also sees a few younger chicks.
"Why are you sitting on your parent's feet?"
Barrington asks one of these smaller chicks.
"To stay off of the ice," the chick answers. "It's COLD!"

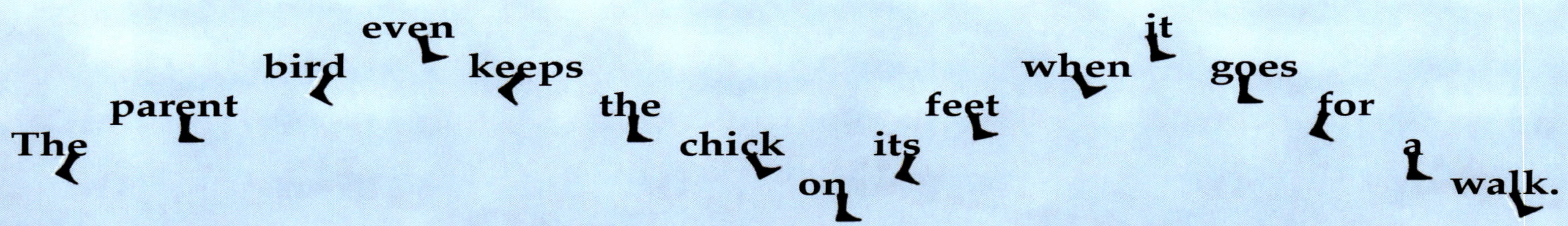

The parent bird even keeps the chick on its feet when it goes for a walk.

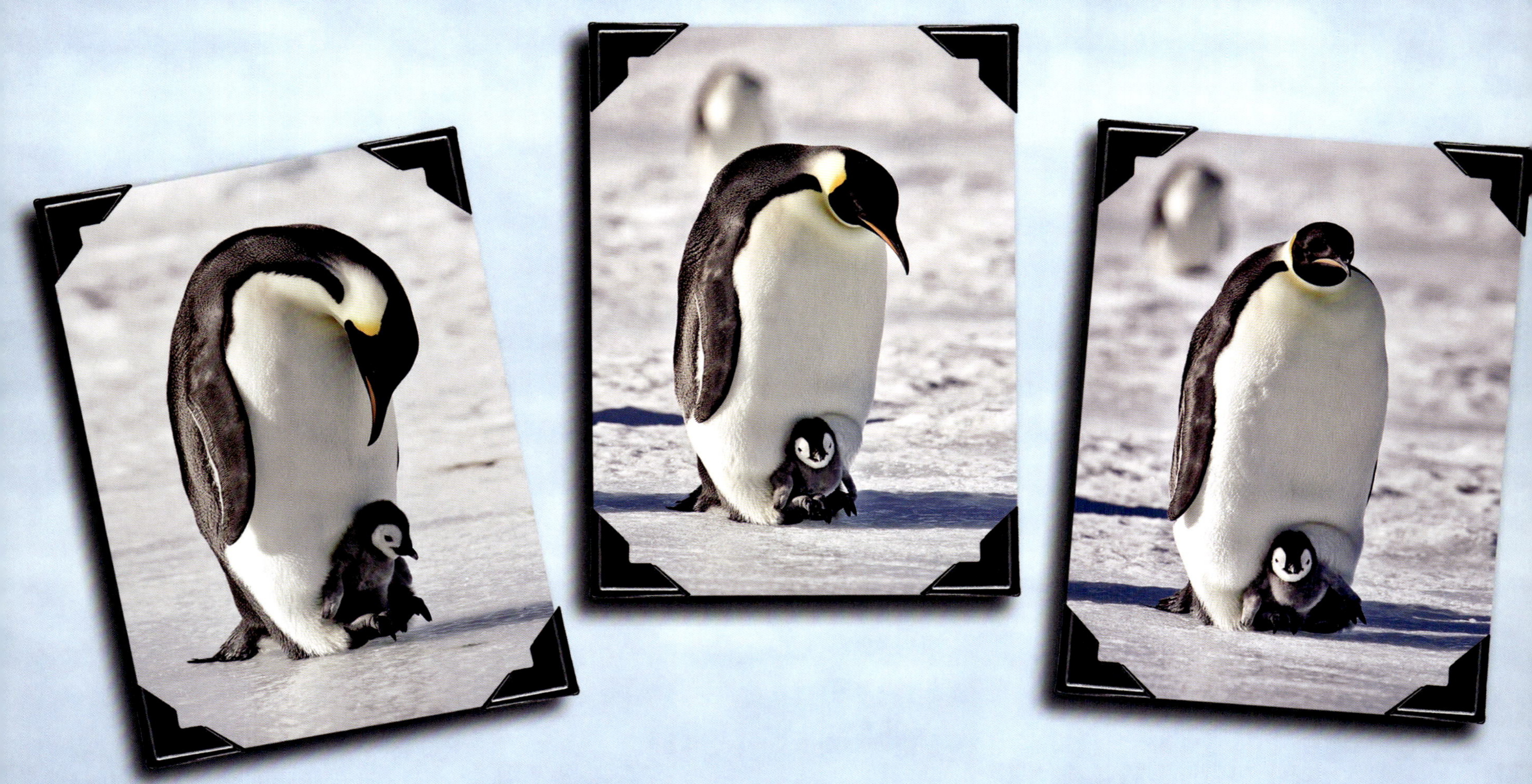

WHAT A FUN RIDE!

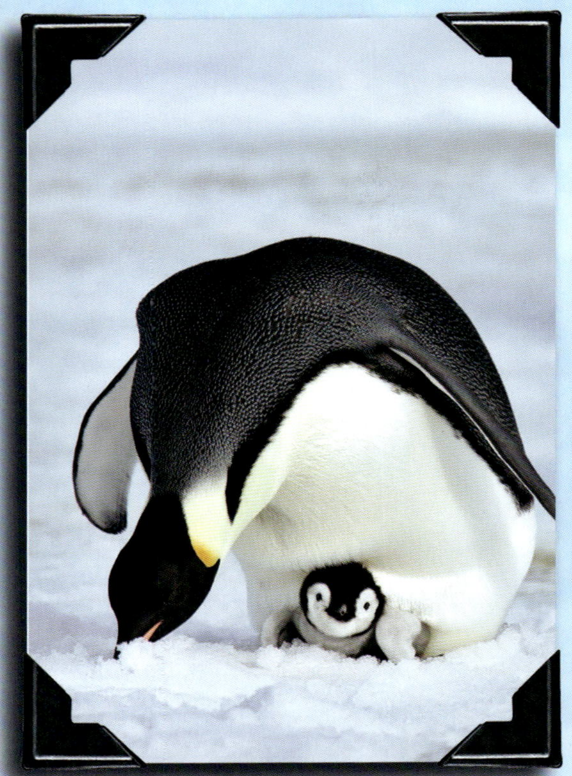

But watch out!
The chick may
also get squashed.

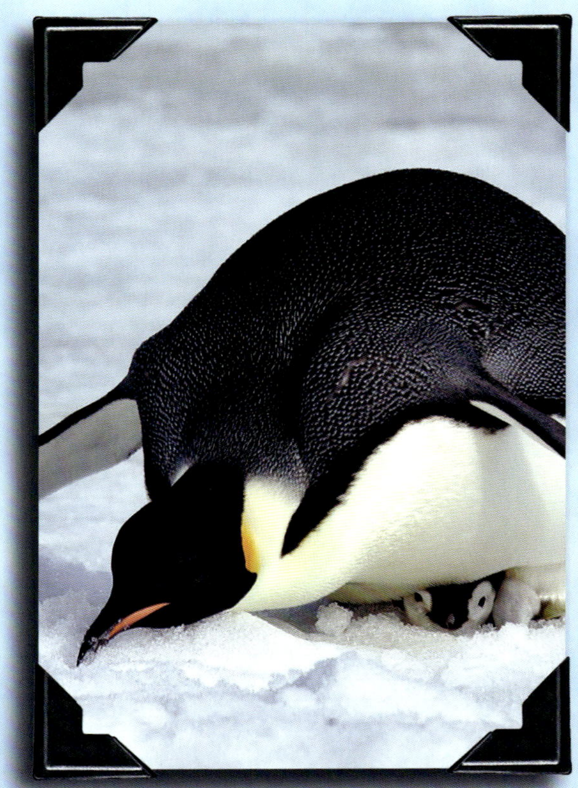

Luckily, the snow
is soft.

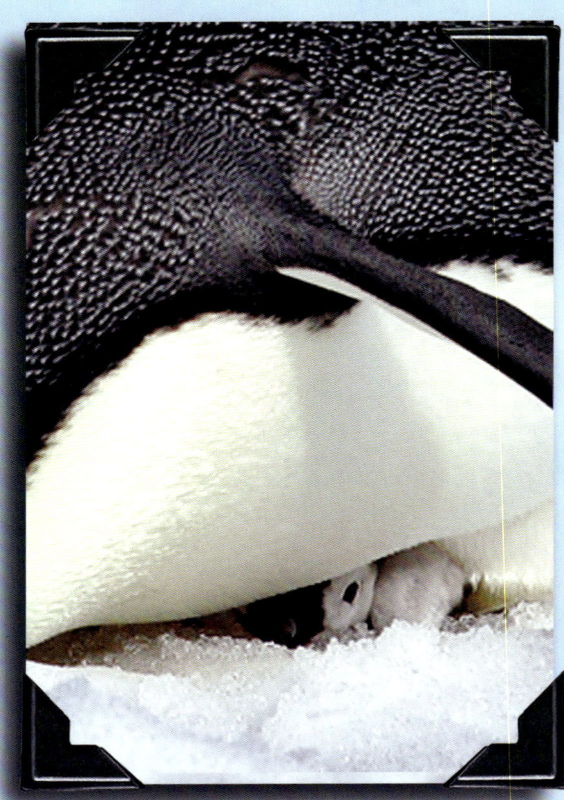

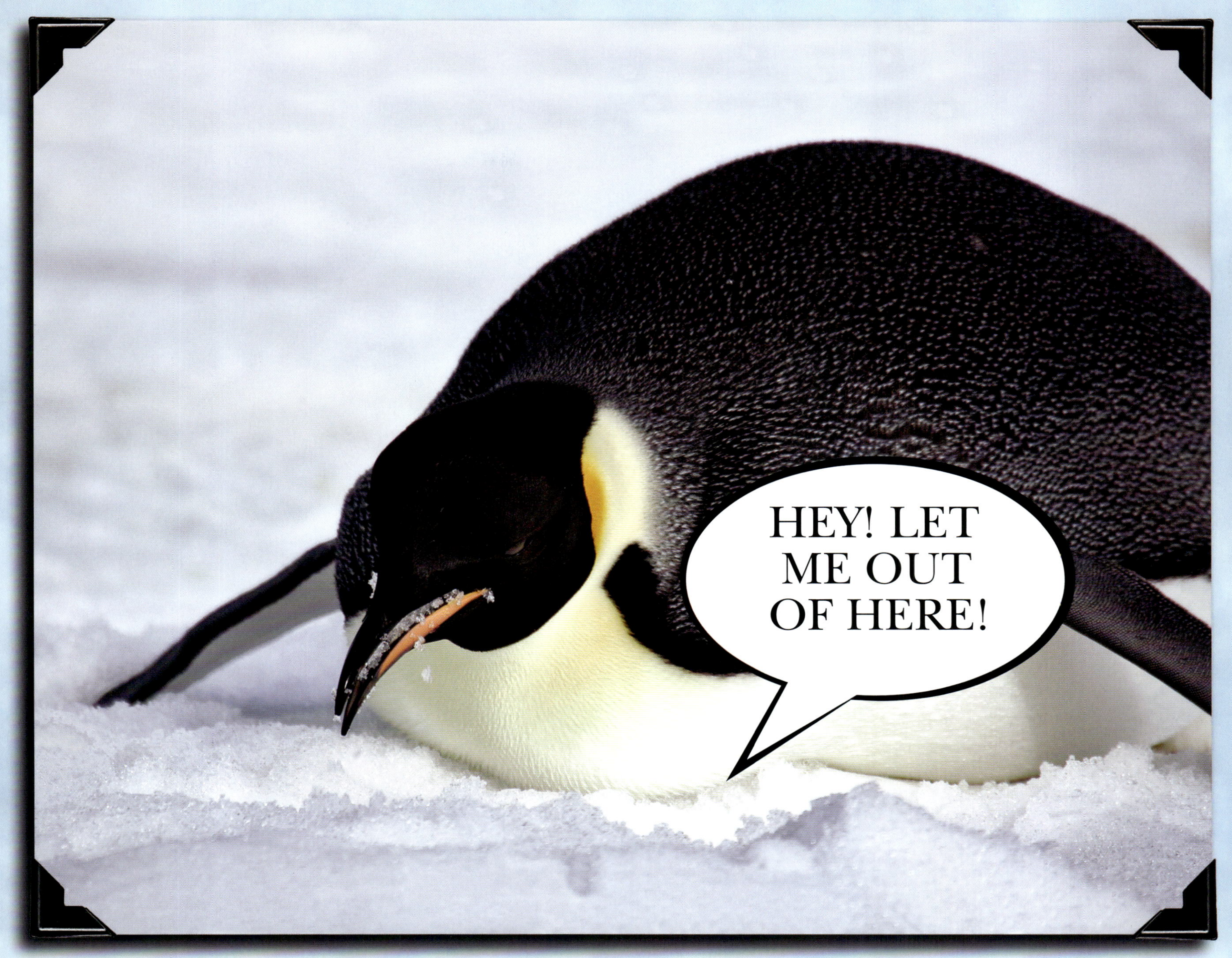
HEY! LET ME OUT OF HERE!

The older chicks are
too big to fit on their
parents' feet.
But they do not
want to give up this warm,
cozy resting place.
They do almost anything
to stay where it is warm.

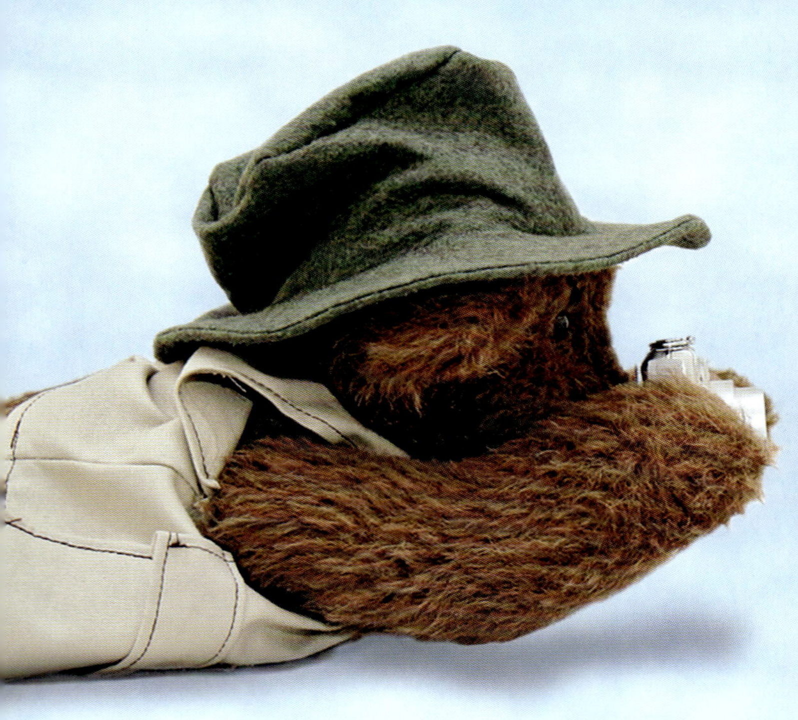

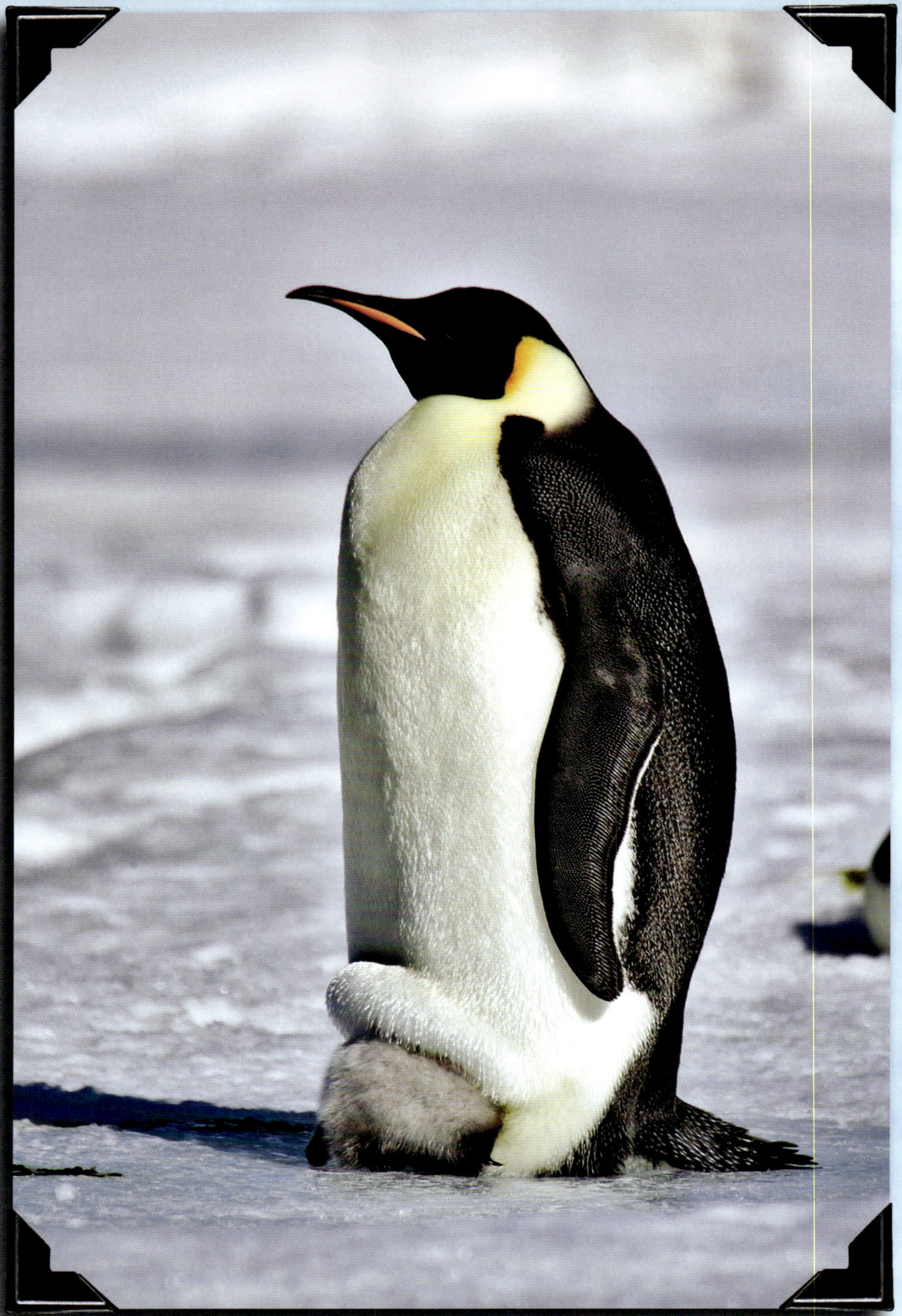

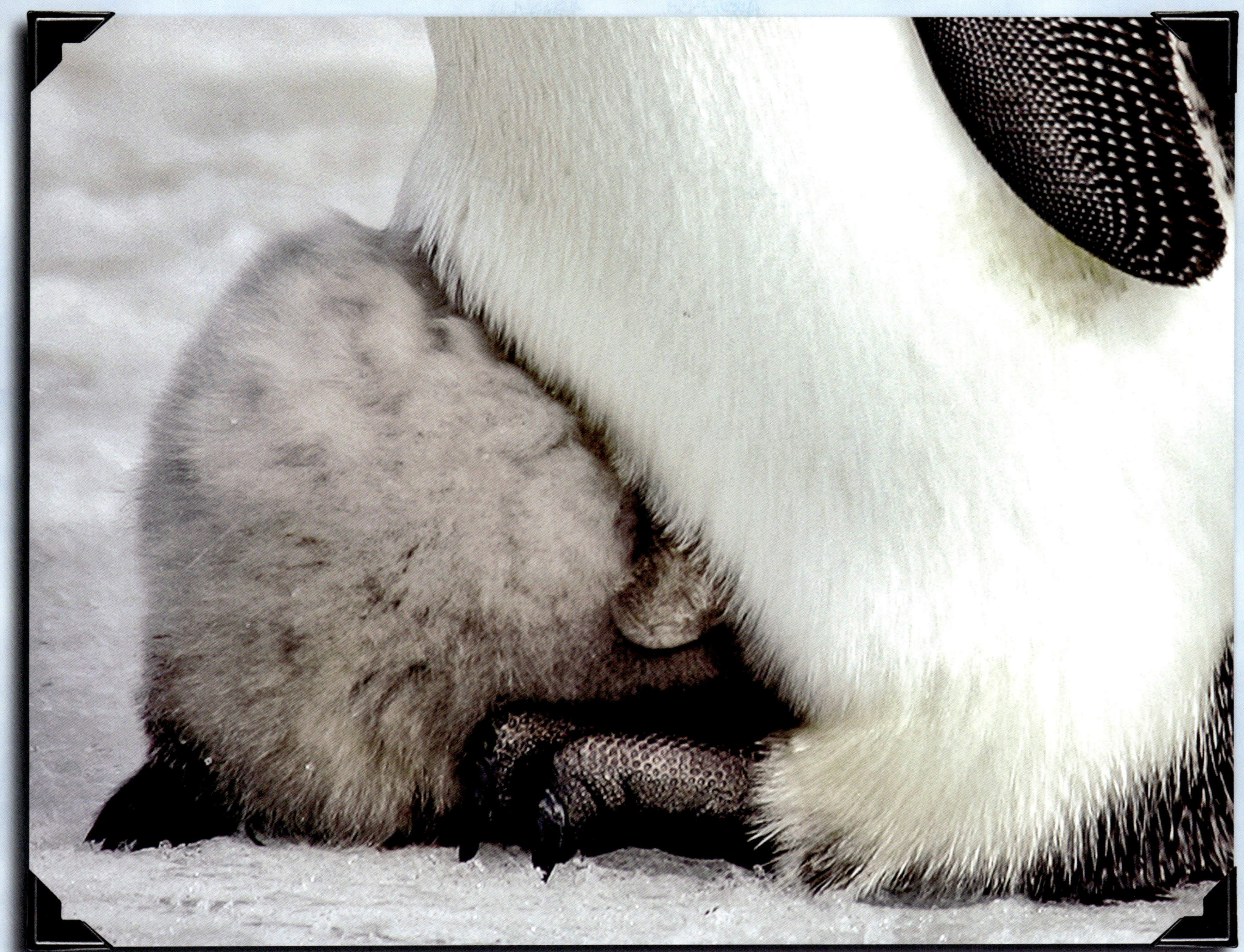

Penguin chicks
are always hungry.
Barrington watches
as a parent feeds
its chick some fish
that it brings up
from its stomach.

"*Eeeyew! That's awful!*"
thinks Barrington.

But the chicks love it.

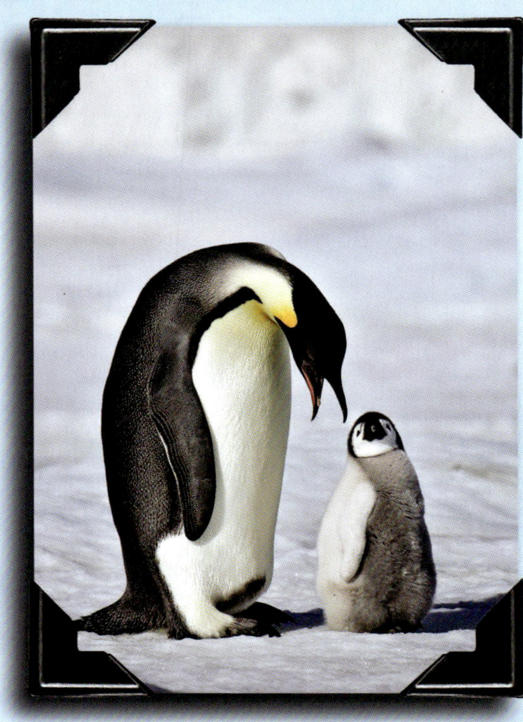

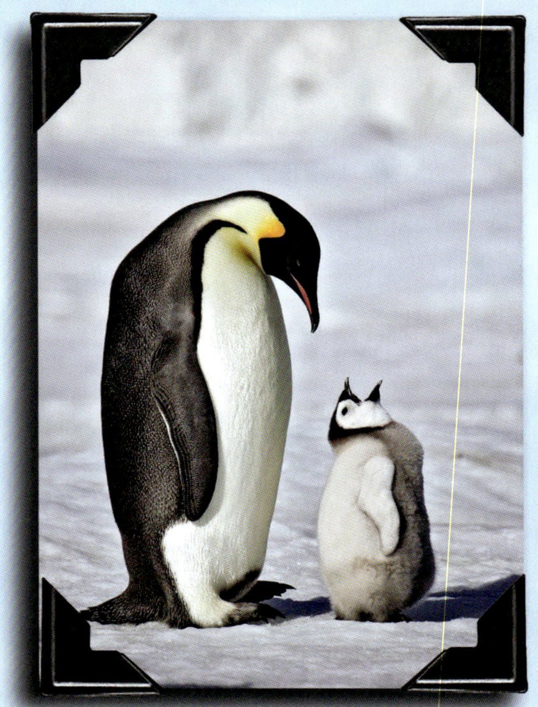

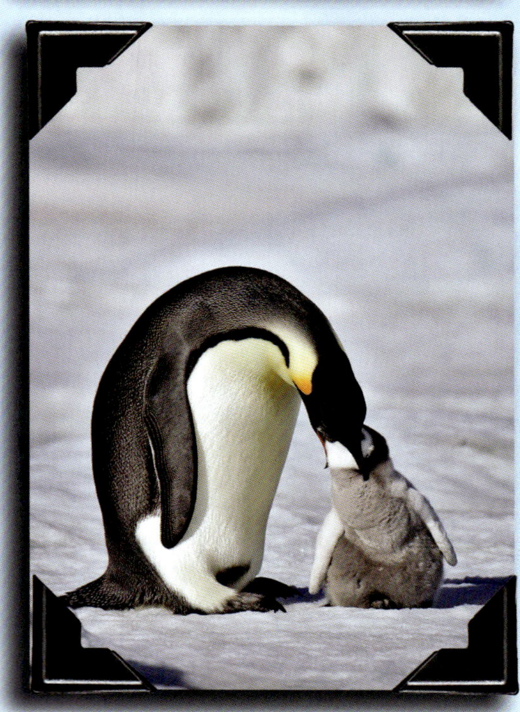

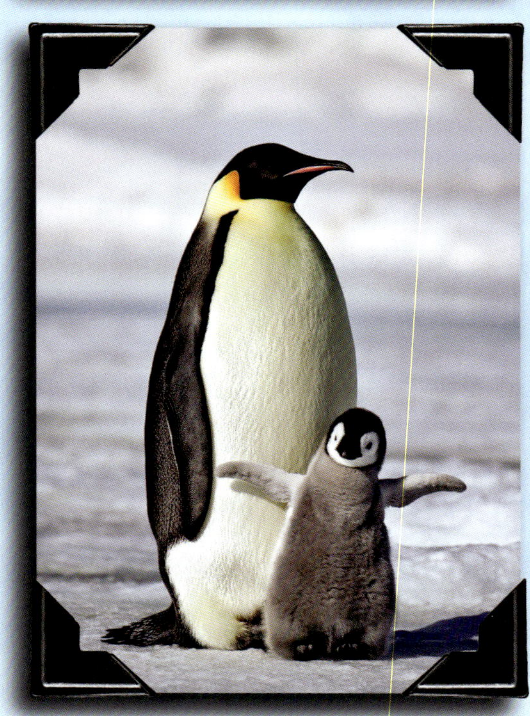

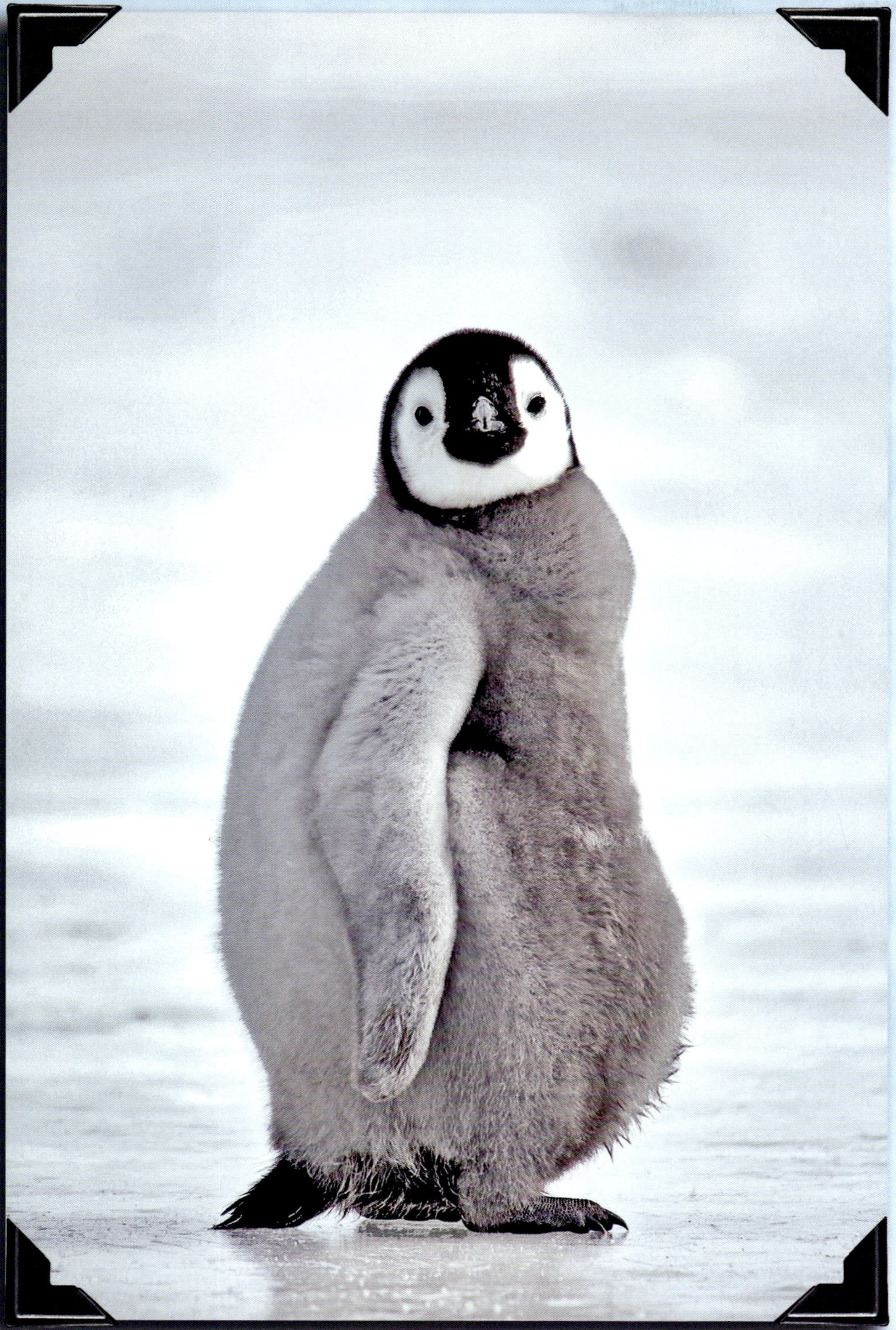

It makes them grow fat and strong.

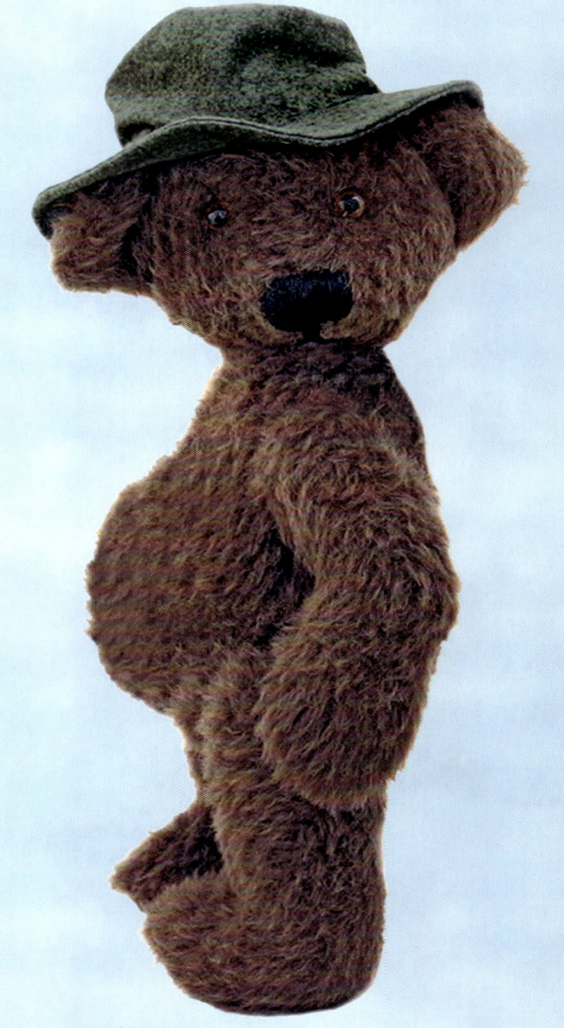

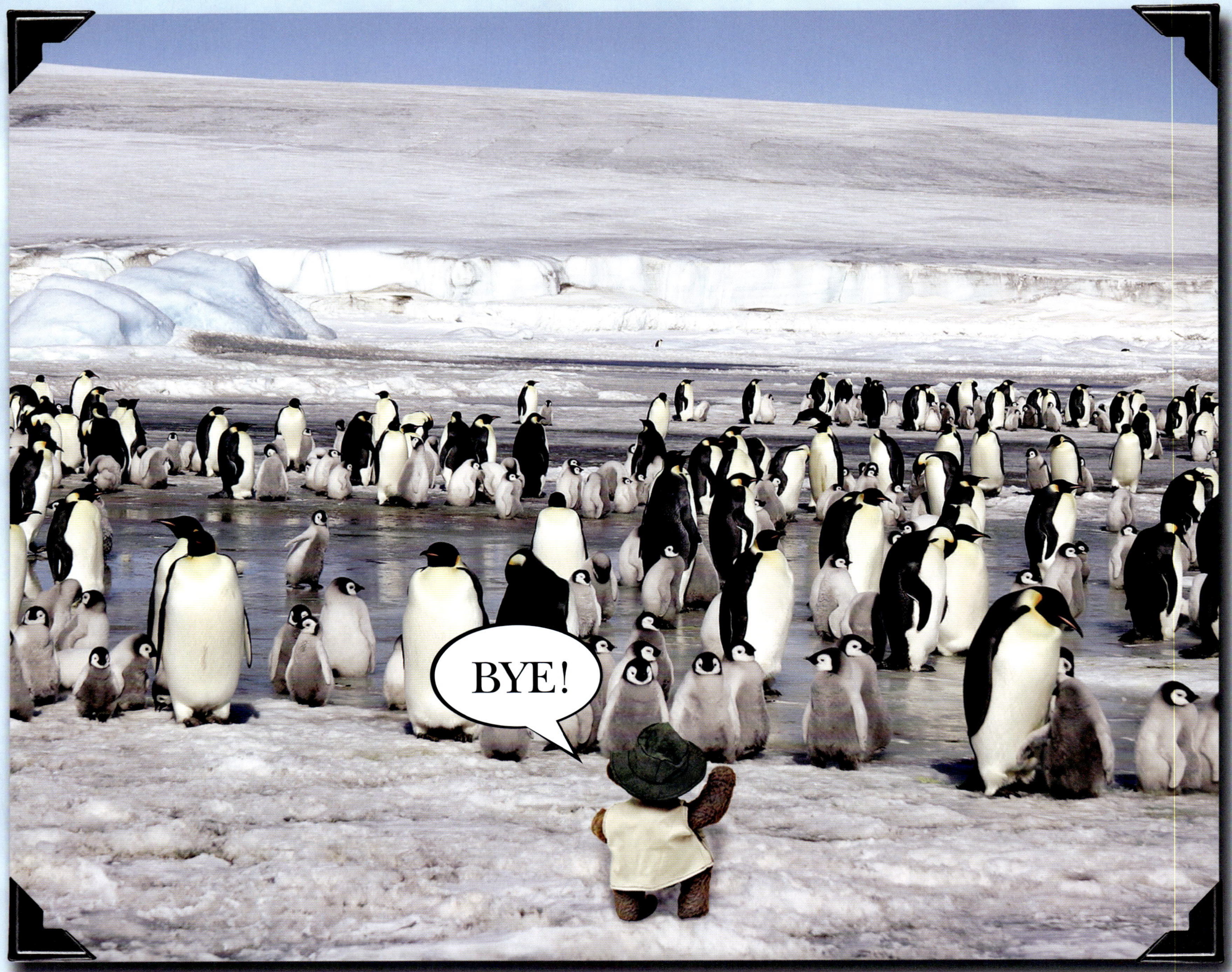
BYE!

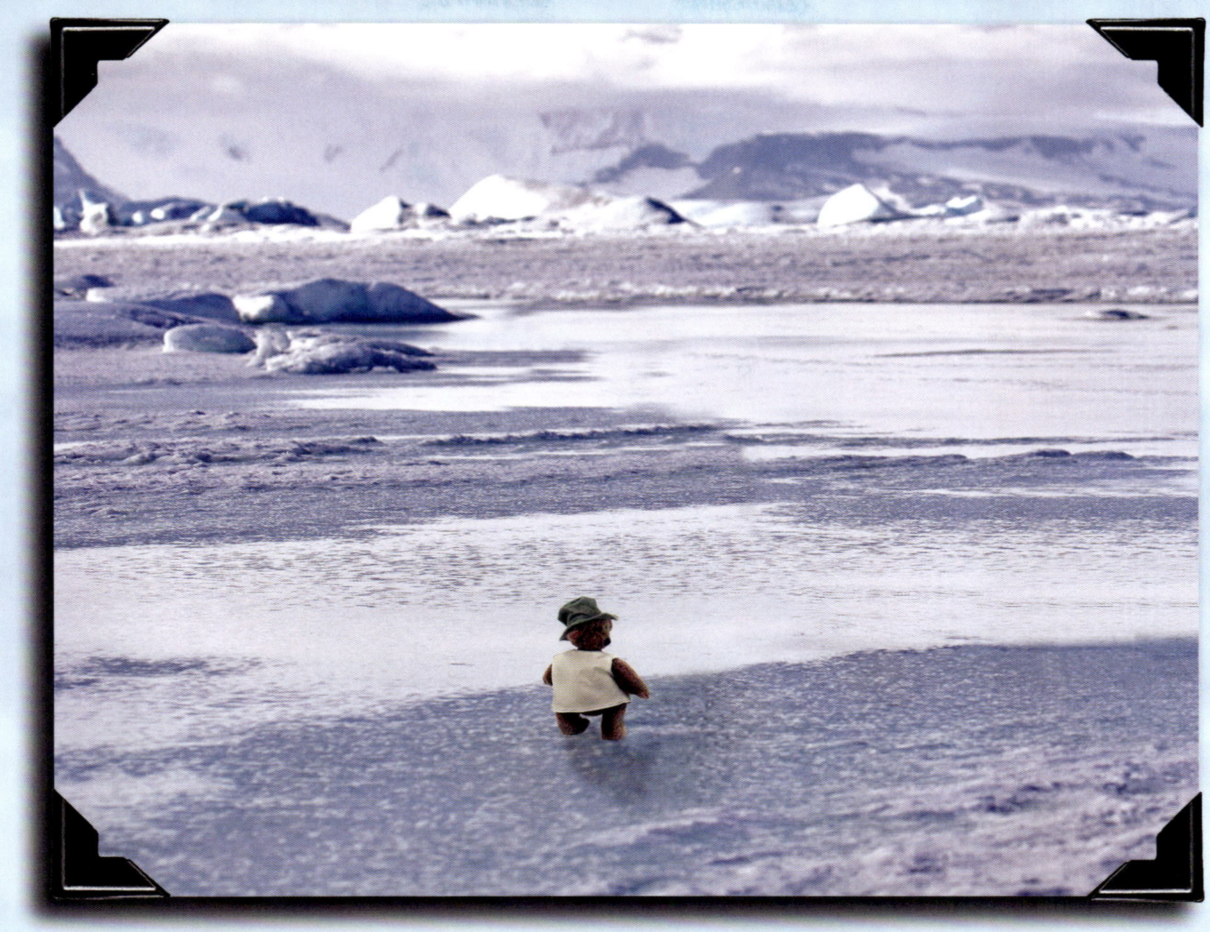

All too soon it is time to leave Antarctica.

Barrington Bear enjoyed his visit with the Emperors. He learned many interesting things. He took a lot of cool pictures. Best of all, he had lots of fun! Now it is time to say goodbye to all of his new friends. Barrington must begin the long journey home.

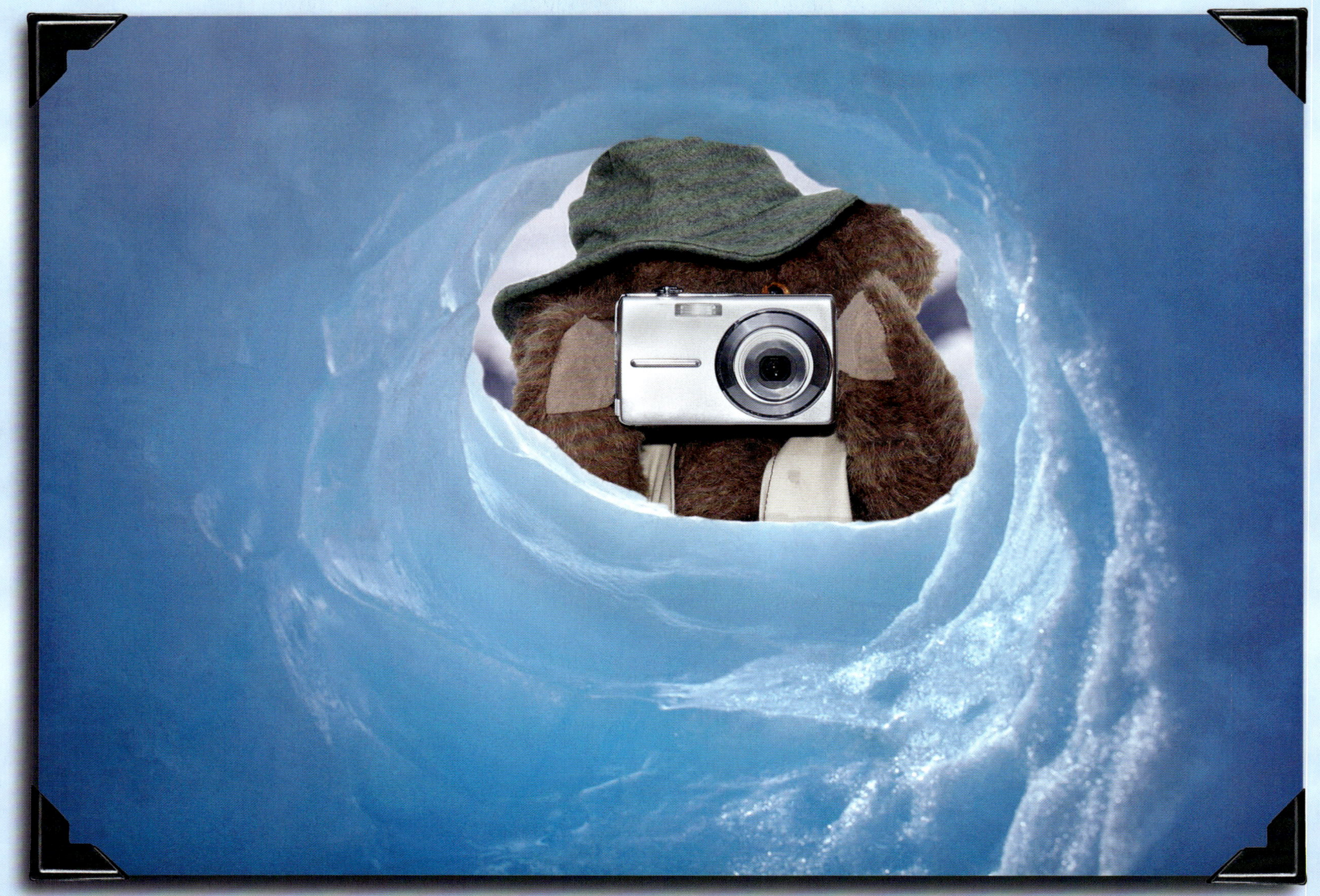

"Maybe just one more picture!"

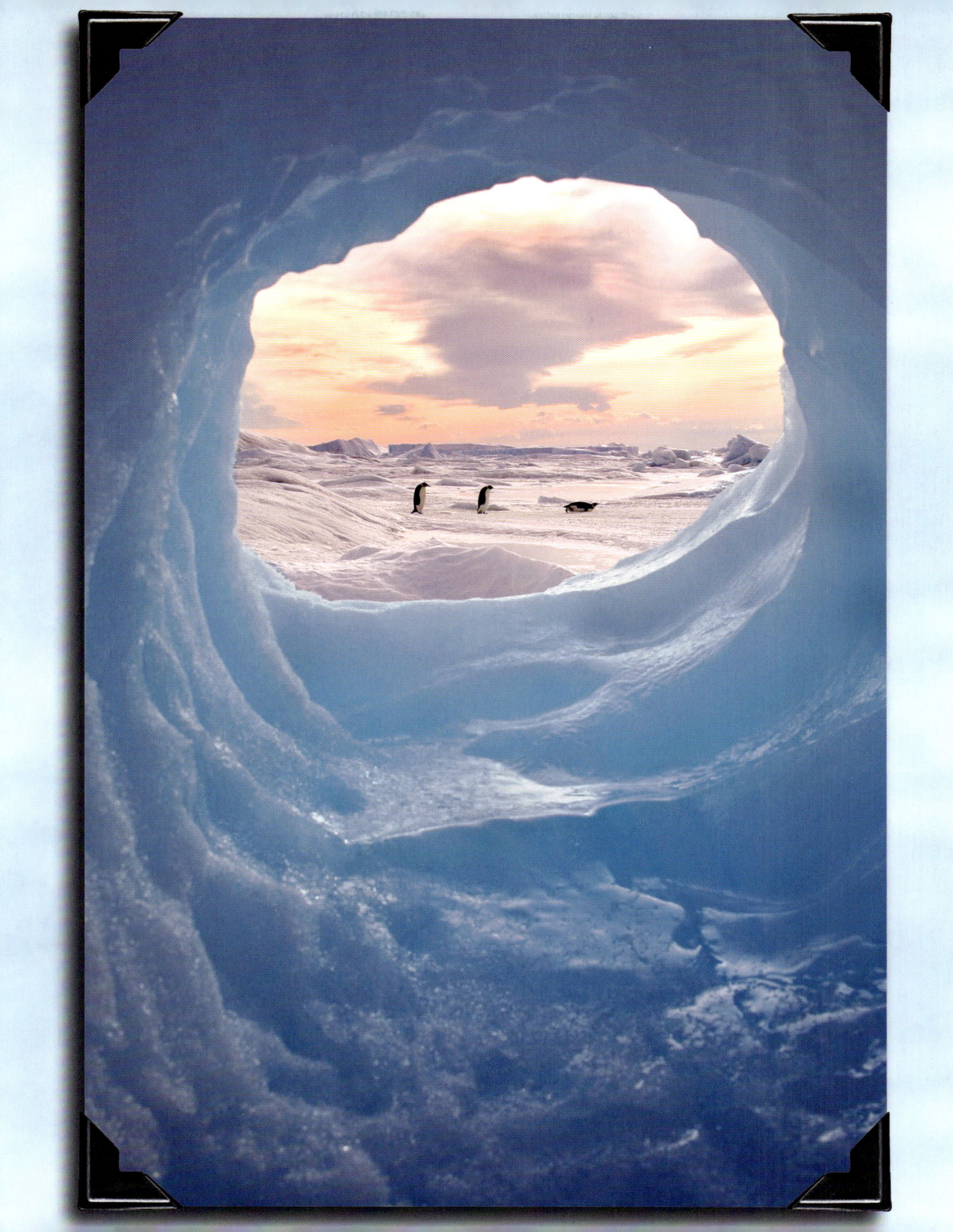

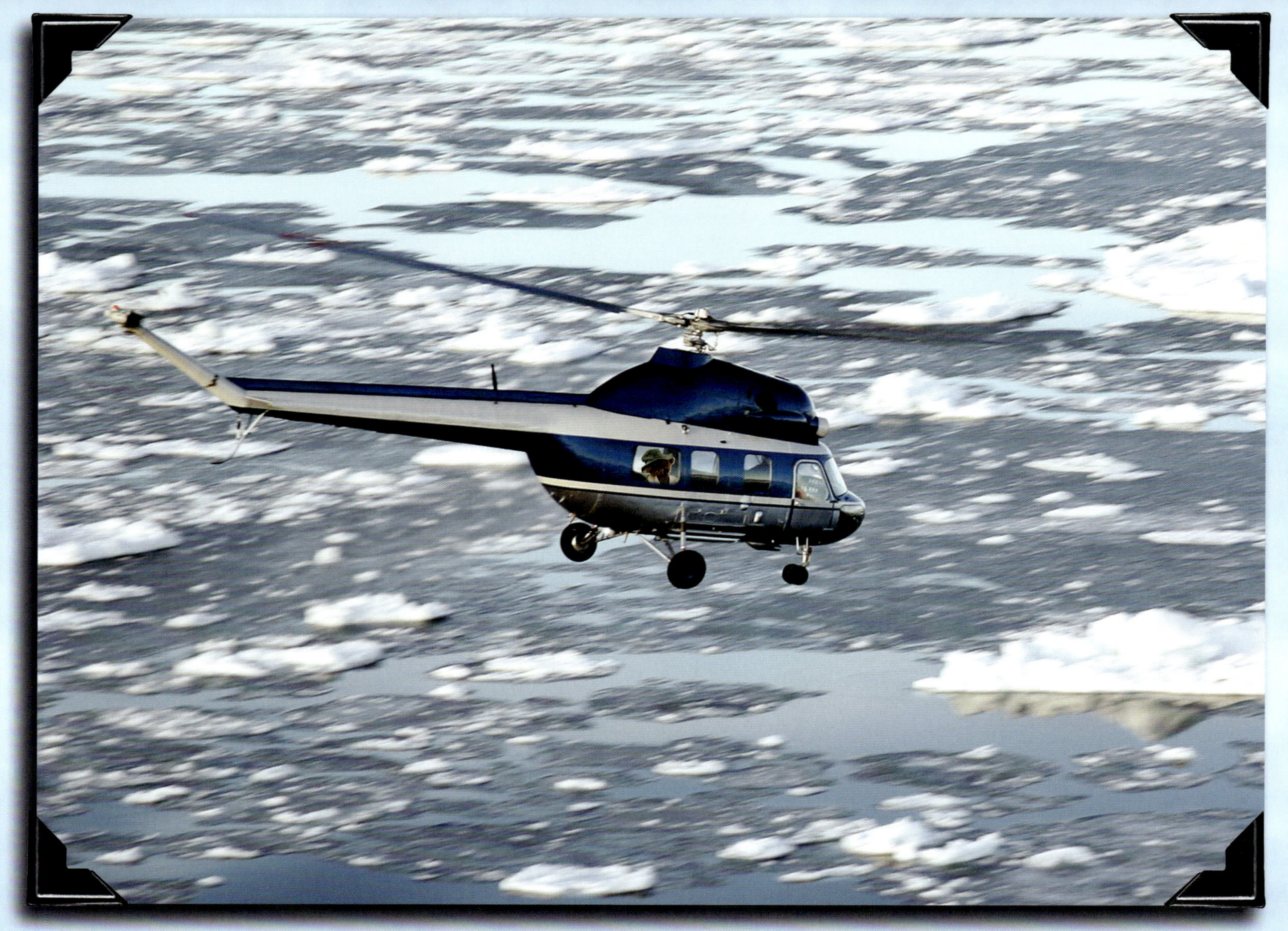

Barrington likes traveling around the world and seeing new places.
He enjoys making new friends and trying new things.
But Barrington Bear…

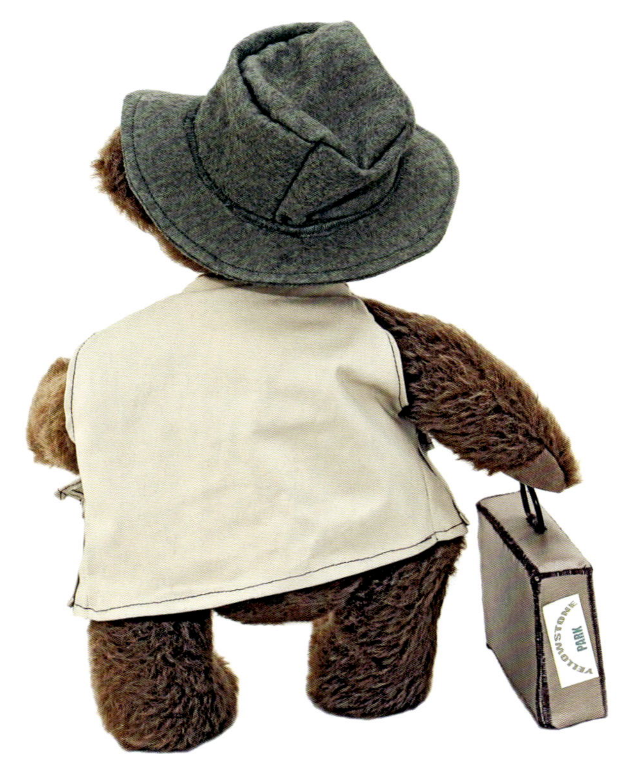

… always likes traveling home best.

"I hope you enjoyed the trip to Antarctica.

On my next trip I will be going on safari in Africa. Please join me for another exciting adventure.

I really like having you along. Goodbye for now."

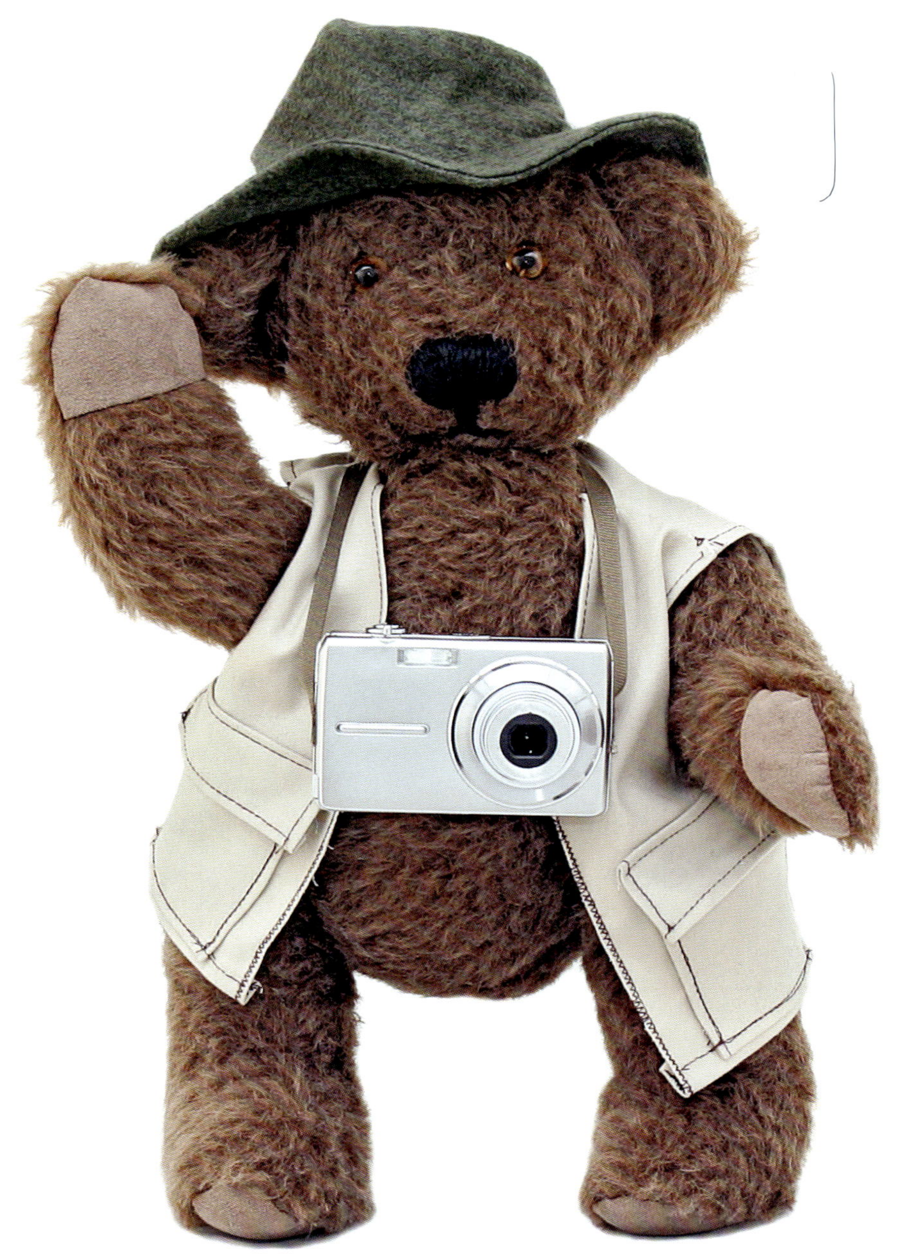

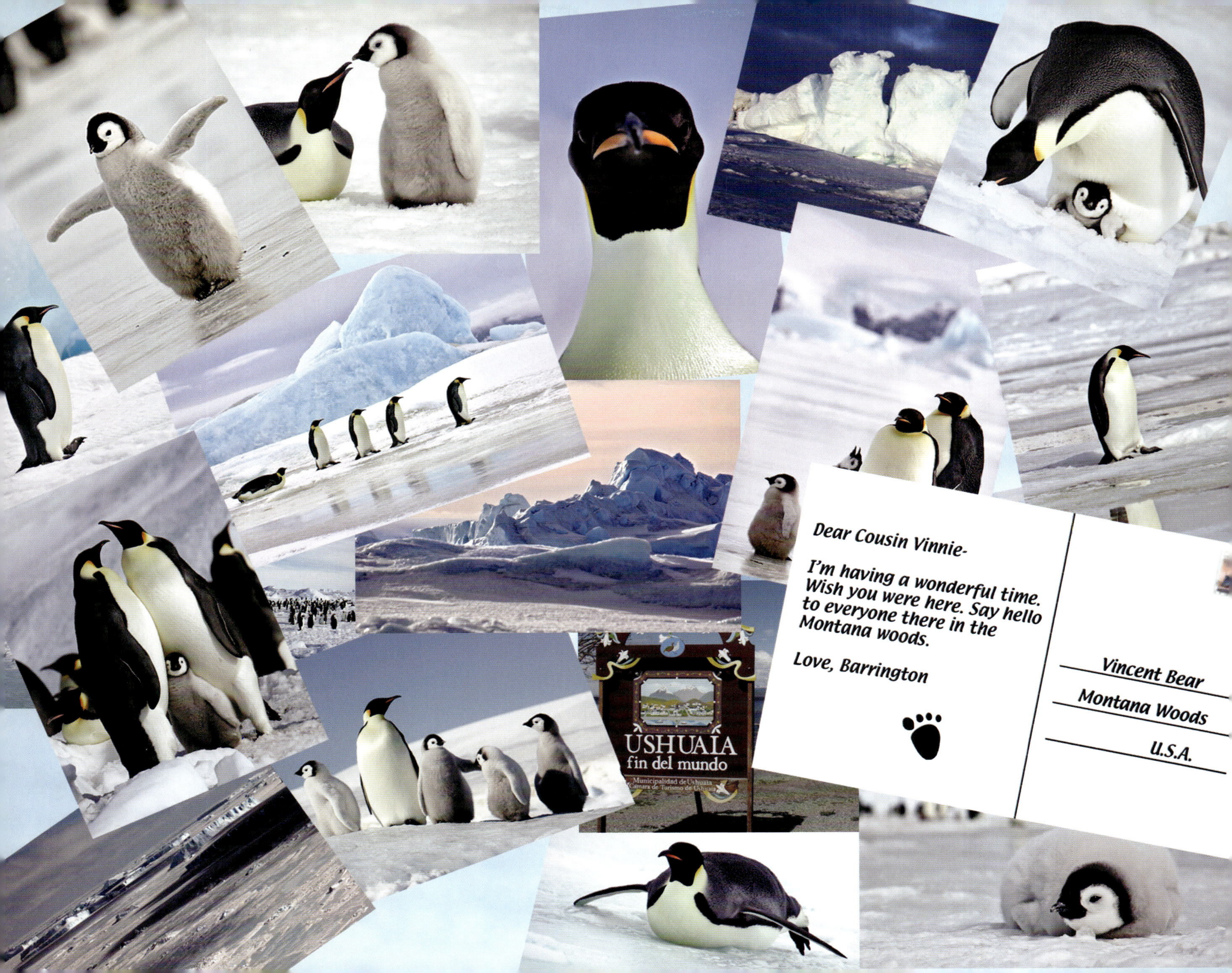
Dear Cousin Vinnie-
I'm having a wonderful time. Wish you were here. Say hello to everyone there in the Montana woods.
Love, Barrington
Vincent Bear
Montana Woods
U.S.A.
USHUAIA
fin del mundo
Municipalidad de Ushuaia
Cámara de Turismo de Ushuaia

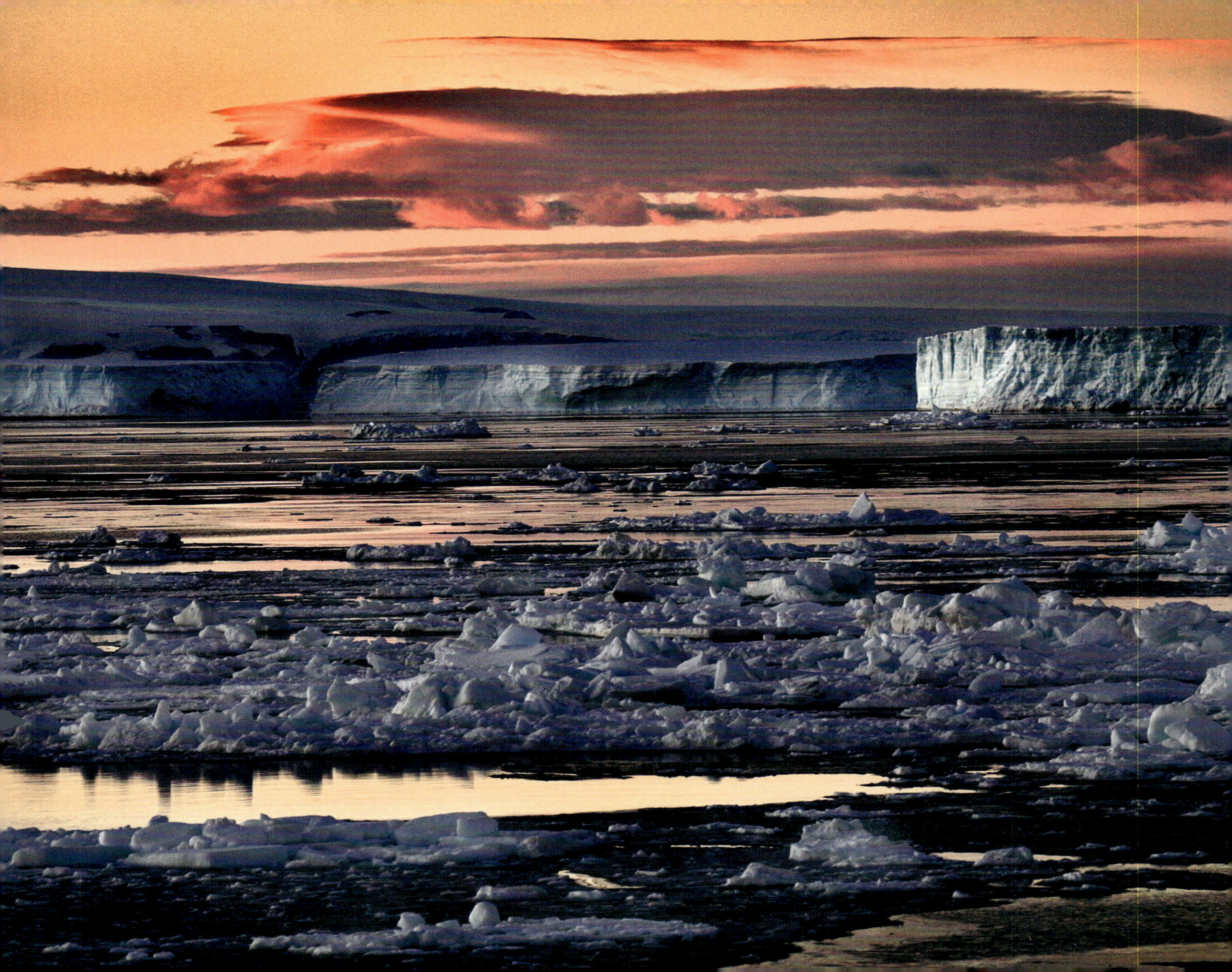

Glossary

ANTARCTICA	A large island continent at the bottom of the Earth.
BROOD PATCH	A spot on a birds stomach with no feathers. Used to keep eggs and chicks warm.
COLONY	A group of animals or birds.
CRÉCHE	The name for a grouping of young animals. It is a French word meaning 'infant bed'.
ICEBREAKER	A very strong and powerful ship. It is used for sailing through the ice on top of the frozen sea.
INCUBATE	To keep warm.
PREENING	To smooth and clean hair or feathers.

Emperor Penguin Facts

- There are 17 species of penguins worldwide.
- The Emperor penguin is the world's largest penguin.
- Emperor penguins grow to be over 40 inches tall. They can weigh 80 pounds.
- The Emperor lays a single egg in the middle of the Antarctic winter. Temperatures can fall below -70 degrees Fahrenheit. The wind often blows over 100 miles per hour. The penguins lay and carry their egg on their feet. They cover it with a brood patch to keep it warm
- The male Emperor goes almost 4 months without eating. He is the one that incubates the egg. After laying the egg, the female returns to the ocean to find food.
- Emperor penguins can dive farther and longer than any other bird. They can dive to 700 feet. They can stay under water for 15 minutes at a time.
- Emperor penguins almost never step on land. They nest on the ice and swim in the ocean.
- There are about 400,000 Emperor penguins in the world.
- The scientific name for the Emperor penguin is *Aptenodytes forsteri.*
- Even though they are birds, Emperor penguins cannot fly.

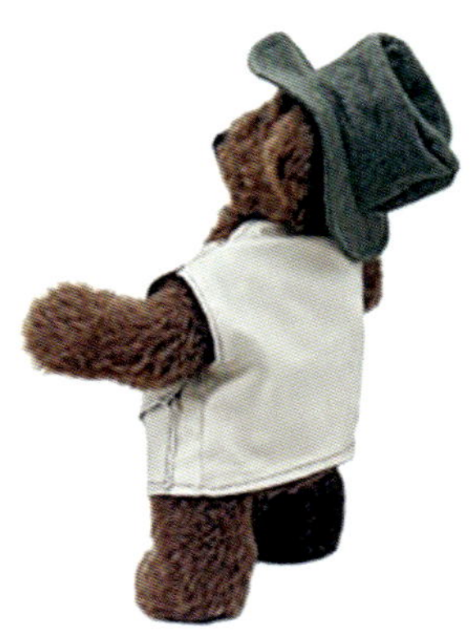

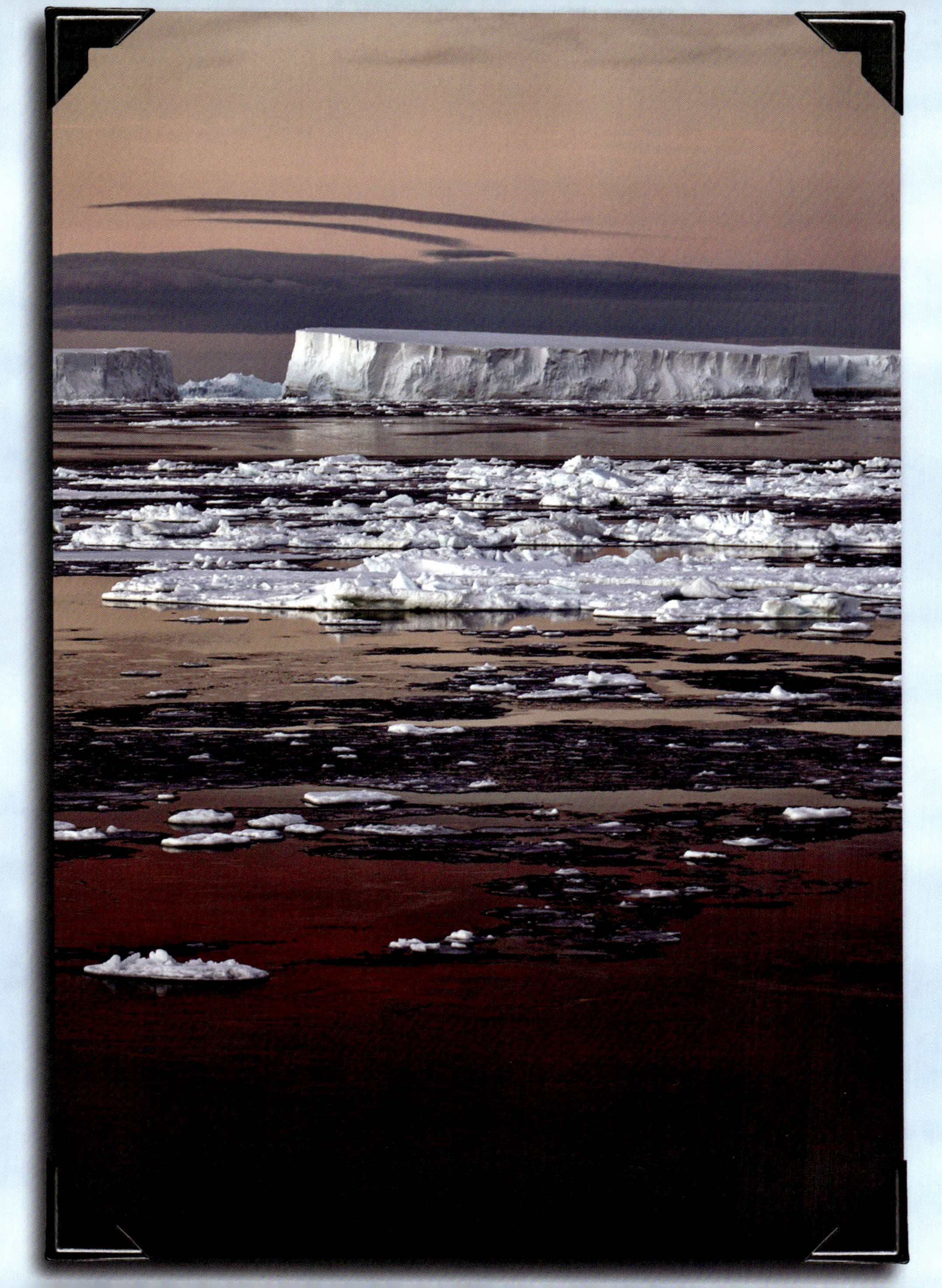

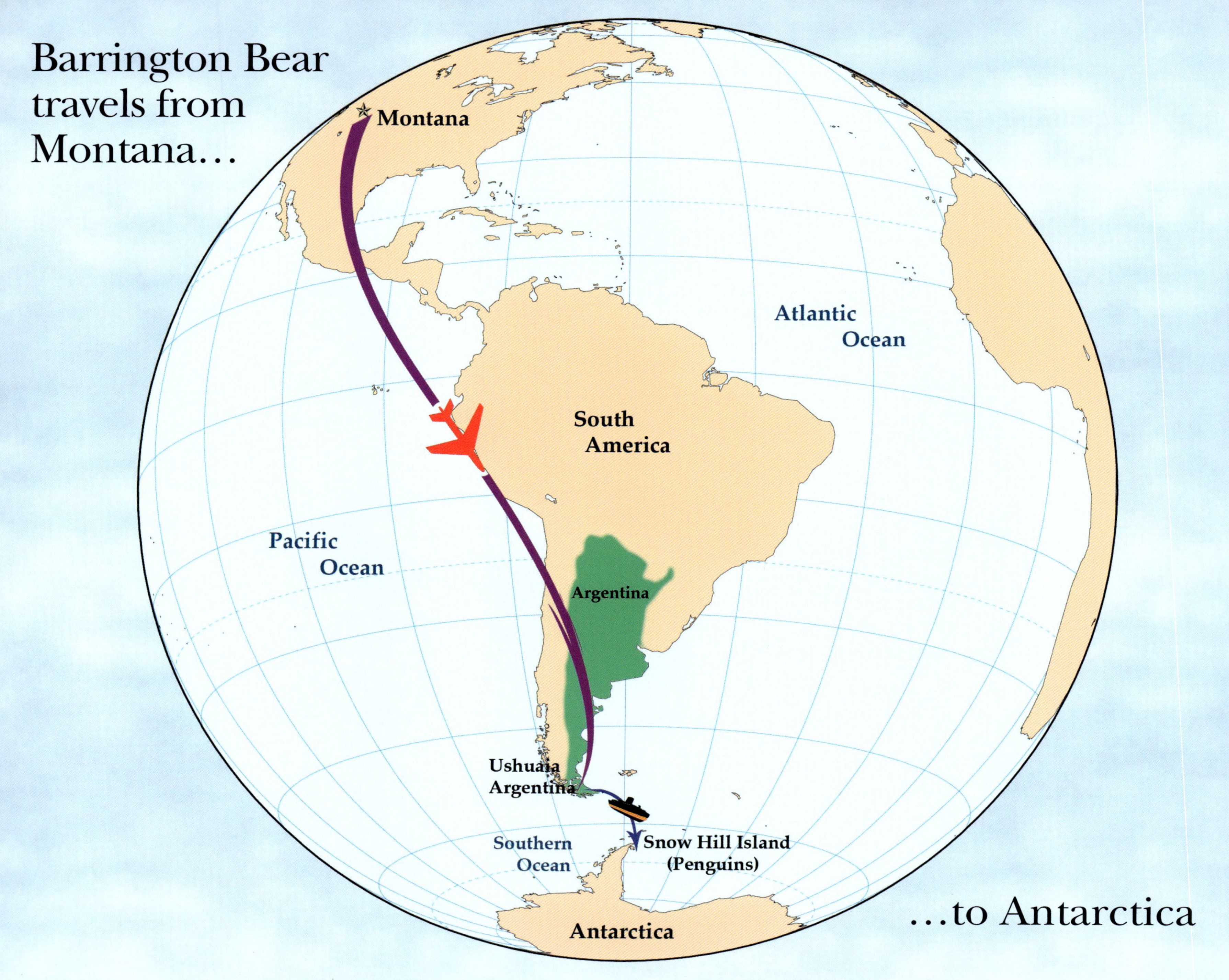

Barrington Bear travels from Montana…
Montana
Atlantic Ocean
South America
Pacific Ocean
Argentina
Ushuaia Argentina
Southern Ocean
Snow Hill Island (Penguins)
Antarctica
…to Antarctica